## CAMBRIDGE
### UNIVERSITY PRESS

# Click Start

# INTERNATIONAL EDITION

## Learner's Book 5

# CAMBRIDGE
## UNIVERSITY PRESS

University Printing House, Cambridge CB2 8BS, United Kingdom

One Liberty Plaza, 20th Floor, New York, NY 10006, USA

477 Williamstown Road, Port Melbourne, VIC 3207, Australia

314–321, 3rd Floor, Plot 3, Splendor Forum, Jasola District Centre, New Delhi – 110025, India

79 Anson Road, #06–04/06, Singapore 079906

Cambridge University Press is part of the University of Cambridge.

It furthers the University's mission by disseminating knowledge in the pursuit of education, learning and research at the highest international levels of excellence.

www.cambridge.org
Information on this title: www.cambridge.org/9781108951883

First published 2021

20  19  18  17  16  15  14  13  12  11  10  9  8  7  6  5  4  3

Printed in Poland by Opolgraf

ISBN 9781108951883 Paperback

# Introduction

The international edition of *Click Start: Computing for Schools* is designed around the latest developments in the field of computer science, information and communication technology. Based on Windows 7 and MS Office 2010, with extensive updates on Windows 10 and MS Office 2016, the series aids the understanding of the essentials of computer science including computer basics, office applications, creative software, programming concepts and programming languages.

Each level of the series has been designed keeping in mind the learning ability of the learners as well as their interests. Efforts have been made to use examples from day-to-day life, which will help the learners to bridge the gap between their knowledge of the subject and the real world. The books are designed to offer a holistic approach and help in the overall development of the learners.

## KEY FEATURES

- **Snap Recap:** Probing questions to begin a chapter and assess pre-knowledge
- **Learning Objectives:** A list of the learning outcomes of the chapter
- **Activity:** Interactive exercise after every major topic to reinforce analytical skills and application-based learning
- **Exercise:** A variety of questions to test understanding
- **Fact File:** Interesting concept-related facts to improve concept knowledge
- **Quick Key** and **Try This:** Shortcuts and useful tips on options available for different operations
- **Glossary:** Chapter-end list of important terms along with their definitions
- **You Are Here:** Quick recap
- **Lab Work:** Practical exercises to enable application of concepts through learning-by-doing
- **Project Work:** Situational tasks to test practical application of the concepts learnt
- **Who Am I?:** Biographies to inspire young learners
- **Sample Paper:** Practice and preparation for exams

The aim of this book is to make learning fun and to help the learners achieve expertise in this fast-changing world of computer science.

# Overview

**Snap Recap**
Probing questions to begin a chapter and assess pre-knowledge

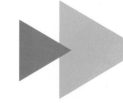
**SNAP RECAP**
1. Think about the different types of computer memory and discuss.
2. Discuss the different uses of multimedia.

**Learning Objectives**
A list of the learning outcomes of the chapter

**LEARNING OBJECTIVES**
*You will learn about:*
- the Input–Process–Output cycle
- the components of a computer network
- different types of computer networks

**Activity**
Interactive exercise after every major topic to reinforce analytical skills and application-based learning

**ACTIVITY**
A. Think about the process of generating a timetable for your subjects. What will be the Input, Processing and Output?
1. **Input** ...........................................................
2. **Processing** ...................................................
3. **Output** .........................................................
B. Suggest examples of at least three machines from your daily life that follow the IPO cycle.

**FACT FILE**
MS Word allows you to protect a document. This restricts others from viewing and editing it. You may also select parts of a document that need to be protected.

**Exercise**
A variety of questions to test understanding

**EXERCISE**
A. **Fill in the blanks.**
1. ........................................ is designed to create a productive and efficient work environment.
2. The Ribbon includes tabs, groups and ..........................
3. Microsoft Word is a tool which is used to create professional-looking ..........................
4. .......................... can be used for calculation, database management and preparation of charts.
5. .......................... is a pictorial representation of data.

**Fact File**
Interesting concept-related snippets to improve concept knowledge

**Quick Key**
and **Try This**
Shortcuts and useful tips on options available for different operations

**QUICK KEY**
For inserting a page number in your document — **Alt + Shift + P**

**TRY THIS**
Open the **Run** dialog box and type **osk**. Click OK. The On-Screen Keyboard will appear on the screen.

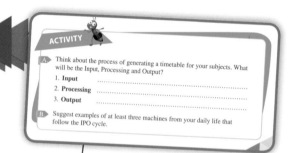

**Glossary**

Chapter-end list of important terms along with their definitions

GLOSSARY

Desktop background  An image used as a background on a computer screen.
Graphical User Interface (GUI)  An interface that uses graphical icons and visual indicators rather than text.
Multitasking  The ability to do more than one thing on a computer at a time.
Theme  A background with a set of sound, icons and other elements that helps you to customise your computer.
Virtual keyboard  A utility program that displays an on-screen keyboard allowing the mouse pointer to type.

YOU ARE HERE 5

1. Formatting and editing of the slides helps to make your presentation more appealing to the audience.
2. Editing a slide involves moving and duplicating text.
3. There are four types of text alignment – Right, Left, Center and Justified.
4. Sometimes you need to write information in the form of lists. These lists can be either in the form of bullets or numbers.
5. Slide Background helps you to change the background color, texture and pattern of the slides in the presentation.
6. Graphics can be used to make a presentation more interesting. They can be inserted into the slides in the form of pictures and Clip Art.
7. The order of the slides can be changed easily. Slides can be rearranged either in the Normal View or the Slide Sorter View.

**You Are Here**

Quick recap

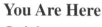

LAB WORK

A. Create a presentation on The Seven Wonders of the World.
B. Create a presentation on parts of a plant.
C. Prepare a presentation on your school. Format slides with slide transitions of your choice. The presentation should focus on the following points.
• Brief introduction about your school
• The buildings of your school
• Educational and other achievements
• Sports facilities
• Any other important information

**Lab Work**

Practical exercises to enable application of concepts through learning-by-doing

PROJECT WORK

Create a list of the students in your class. Ask your subject teachers about all the information they maintain in their register, such as marks, remarks, parental information, parent-teacher's meeting, etc.
Insert that list in MS Excel and use all the formatting you have learnt so far.

**Project Work**

Situational tasks to test practical application of the concepts learnt

WHO AM I?

I was born in England in 1815. As a young girl, I took an interest in mathematics and, in particular, Babbage's work on the analytical engine.
I am considered to be the first computer programmer.
I described how Babbage's analytical engine could be programmed.
I am .............................

**Who Am I?**

Biographies to inspire young learners

Sample **Paper**

Tick (✓) the correct option.

1. Which of the following is not part of a computer network?
   a. Process     b. Server     c. Workstation     d. Transmission cables

2. Identify the correct sentence(s) about a modem used in computer networks.
   a. It stands for modulator demodulator
   b. It converts data from digital to analogue and vice versa for effective transmission.
   c. Both A and B are correct.
   d. Both A and B are incorrect.

3. The ......... option from the Start menu is used for executing a file or application directly.
   a. Accessories     b. All programs     c. Run     d. Gadgets

4. The On-Screen Keyboard is an important utility program. It is also known as:
   a. Online keyboard
   b. Virtual keyboard
   c. Offline keyboard
   d. Soft keyboard

5. The Control Panel can be used to change settings for Windows. Which of the following setting options is not available in it?
   a. Keyboard     b. Sound     c. Motherboard     d. Mail

6. The Region and Language icon of the Control Panel is used for changing the settings of ..........
   a. the display of languages     b. time     c. date     d. All of these

140

**Sample Paper**

Practice and preparation for exams

# C🌐ntents ▶▶

# Know Your Computer

## LEARNING OBJECTIVES

*You will learn about:*

- the Input–Process–Output cycle
- the components of a computer network
- different types of computer networks

## Introduction

The computer is an electronic device capable of solving problems by accepting data, performing operations on the data, and giving a result. Let us revisit the concepts of input, process and output.

## Input

**Input** is the raw data given to the computer using input devices like the keyboard, mouse and scanner.

Just as you put dirty clothes in a washing machine, you input the raw data into a computer.

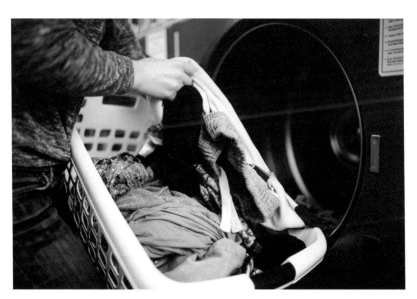

*Input*

## Process

The raw data is manipulated to generate information by performing certain operations using the computer's processing device, the Central Processing Unit. It is similar to the processing of dirty clothes in the washing machine.

*Processing of input*

*Output*

## Output

The information generated is known as **output**. The output information is given with the help of output devices like the printer and monitor. It is similar to clean clothes, after processing.

## The Input–Process–Output (IPO) cycle

The three terms 'input', 'process' and 'output' are interrelated. The information flows from the input device to the processing device and then to the output device. This whole flow of information follows a cycle known as the Input–Process–Output (IPO) cycle. This cycle presents the information in a user-friendly way.

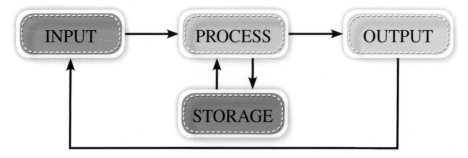

*The Input–Process–Output cycle*

Information often needs to be kept safe for later use. This information may be stored in storage devices like compact discs (CDs), hard disks, flash drives and memory cards.

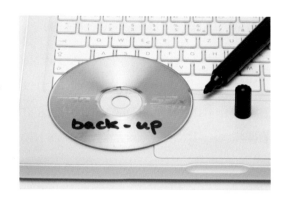

*Storage device*

Let us study the IPO cycle through the example given below.

## Playing games

1. **Input**: The player's information given to the computer along with keys pressed to run the animations.

2. **Process**: The speed and direction of the animations are controlled by pressing different keys.

3. **Output**: The effect of pressing different keys is seen as animations and sound on the screen.

*A child playing a computer game*

## ACTIVITY

A. Think about the process of generating a timetable for your subjects. What will be the Input, Processing and Output?

1. **Input** ...............................................................................

2. **Processing** ...............................................................................

3. **Output** ...............................................................................

B. Suggest examples of at least three machines from your daily life that follow the IPO cycle.

# Computer Networks

The word 'network' may be defined as a collection of computers connected together for the purpose of sharing information and resources. For example, sharing one printer among ten computers through a network is an example of resource sharing. These interconnected computers may be within a local area or may cross different cities or countries.

*Networking concept*

Computers cannot communicate with each other locally or remotely without computer networking. Just imagine a bank or an office without computer networking! How difficult it would be for the employees to communicate and share data.

In today's world, networking is essential in bank transactions through ATMs, online ticketing and reservations, online shopping, etc.

## Advantages of networking

Computer networking is needed for the following reasons.

1. **Limited resources**: Instead of connecting a printer to all the computers separately, you can connect it to the main network. In this way, every computer can share the printer.

2. **Sharing information**: Information is centralised and can be made available to all the computers connected to a network.

3. **Lower costs**: It reduces cost, as an input device like a scanner and an output device like a printer can be easily shared.

## Components of a computer network

The different parts of a computer network are shown on a diagram on the next page.

1. **Workstations**: The individual computers connected to a network to share data and information are called **workstations** or **terminals**. They can be compared to professionals working together in a group or in a department to do a specific job.

2. **Server**: The main computer that controls the functioning of the entire network is called the **server**. It can be compared to a manager of a company who manages all the work and communicates with the executives.

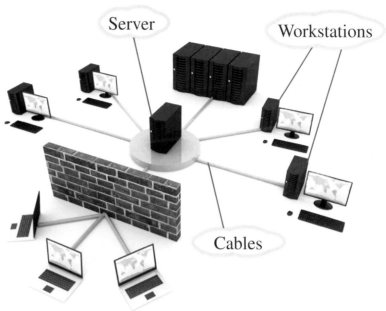

Server    Workstations

Cables

*Parts of a computer network*

3. **Communication channels**: These are used to connect the computers in the network to allow the computers to communicate with each other. These channels can be cables, fiber optics, radio waves or satellites.

4. **Modem**: This stands for **modulator demodulator**. A modem is an electronic device which allows one computer to send information to another through standard telephone wires and over long distances. It is required because computers are digital devices and the telephone system is analogue. The modem converts digital (binary) data to analogue (continuous) data and vice versa for effective transmission. They can be fitted inside the computer (**internal modem**) or placed outside the computer (**external modem**).

**a.** *Internal modem*    **b.** *External modem*

*Types of modem*

**FACT FILE**

The speed of a modem is calculated in bits per second (bps).

5. **Router**: An electronic device that connects two or more networks and directs the data between them.

6. **Bluetooth**: A system for connecting electronic devices, such as mobile phones and computers, to each other and to the internet using radio signals. To use this technology, a **Bluetooth** device is used. For example, Bluetooth mobile phone headsets.

*A router*

## Types of Network

### Personal Area Network (PAN)

When the computers and devices that belong to the same user are interconnected over a short range, it forms a **Personal Area Network (PAN)**.

*A Bluetooth mobile phone headset*

The communication channels in this case are mainly Bluetooth and Wi-Fi devices.

For example, your desktop PC, mobile phone and laptop connected to the wireless network at your home is an example of a PAN.

### Local Area Network (LAN)

When the computers are interconnected in the same office building, school or home for sharing information, then it forms a **Local Area Network (LAN)**.

A LAN connects computers over a relatively short distance. It generally uses cables as a communication channel.

*PAN*

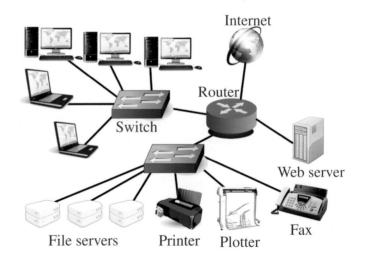

File servers   Printer  Plotter  Fax

*LAN*

## Metropolitan Area Network (MAN)

When the computers are interconnected over an entire city, this forms a **Metropolitan Area Network (MAN)**. For example, all the branches of a company are interconnected using a MAN within the same city.

The cable operator supplies the cable television network using a MAN. The communication channel in this case is either cables or satellites.

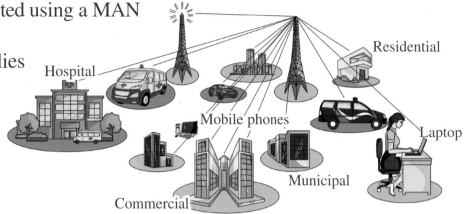

*Metropolitan Area Network*

## Wide Area Network (WAN)

When computers are interconnected for transmitting information over a large geographical area such as a country, a continent or even the whole world, it forms a **Wide Area Network (WAN)**. The internet is the best example of a WAN. Satellite is generally used as a communication channel.

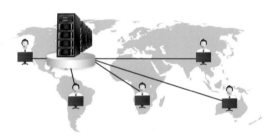

*Wide Area Network*

**ACTIVITY**

A.  Find out which category of network is used in your computer lab.

B.  With the help of your teacher, prepare a PowerPoint presentation on the parts of a computer network.

C.  Double-click on the Network icon on the desktop of your computer. It will give you a list of the computers connected to your network. Discuss the types of network available in your school and the terminals connected to it.

## GLOSSARY

**Computer network**   A network of computers, connected together for sharing information and resources.

**Input**   The raw data given to a computer.

**Internet**   'Internet' stands for 'Interconnected network'. It is a huge network of computers that allows the sharing of data communication services – for example, email.

**IPO cycle**   The flow of information from input devices to processing devices to output devices. IPO stands for 'Input-Process-Output'.

**LAN**   'Local Area Network'. A type of network that connects computers over a relatively short distance.

**MAN**   'Metropolitan Area Network'. A type of network where computers are interconnected to extend over an entire city.

**Modem**   An electronic device which allows one computer to send information to another through telephone wires and over long distances.

**Output**   The processed data generated by a computer.

**PAN**   'Personal Area Network'. A type of network that connects devices that belong to the same user over a short range.

**Process**   Manipulating raw data using a CPU.

**Server**   The main computer that controls the functioning of an entire network.

**WAN**   'Wide area network'. A type of network where computers are interconnected over a large geographical area, like whole countries or the world.

**Workstation**   Individual computers on a computer network.

**YOU ARE HERE**

**1**

1. The computer is an electronic device capable of solving a problem by accepting data, performing operations on the data and giving the result.

2. The information flows from an input device to the processing device and then to an output device. This flow of information follows a cycle, which is known as the Input–Process–Output cycle.

3. Computer networking is needed to share resources, share information and reduce costs.

4. You need workstation(s), a server, a communication channel and a modem to form a network.

5. PAN, LAN, MAN and WAN are common types of network.

EXERCISE

## A. Fill in the blanks.

1. The three terms input, .............................. and output are interrelated.

2. The collection of computers connected together for the purpose of sharing information and resources is called a ............................... .

3. The main computer that controls the functioning of the entire network is called the ............................... .

4. Modem stands for ......................................... .

5. The speed of a modem is calculated in .............................. .

## B. True of false?

1. A WAN connects computers over a relatively short distance.

2. When computers are interconnected to extend over an entire city, then it forms a MAN.

3. The internet is the best example of a PAN.

4. Internet stands for interrelated network.

5. Networking is the solution to limited resources and cost reduction.

## C. Explain the difference between the following:

1. Server and workstation
2. PAN and LAN
3. Input and output
4. WAN and MAN

## D. Give one word for each of the following:

1. The main computer on a network ................................
2. Modulator demodulator ................................
3. A computer on a network ................................
4. Information flow cycle ................................
5. Connects two or more networks ................................

## E. Answer the following questions.

1. Define the IPO cycle. Give an example.
2. What is the importance of a computer network?
3. What is a modem? State the different types.
4. Name the four types of network.
5. On a school network, can you give a print command from ten different computers to one printer? Justify your answer.

## LAB WORK

A. Make a list of places you visit in your daily life where you see networking being used.

B. Find out the type of network used in your school computer lab. Make a note of it and find out which other network can be used there.

C. Communication channels are used to interconnect computers. These are WIRED and WIRELESS channels. Use the internet to find out more about these. Create a PowerPoint presentation to explain these communication channels.

## PROJECT WORK

Design an A4 poster showing any one type of network and the connectivity between the various devices. You can use Paint to create the poster.

# Using Windows

**2**

## SNAP RECAP

1. Define operating system.
2. Explain the difference between a desktop wallpaper and a screen saver.

## LEARNING OBJECTIVES

*You will learn about:*

- advantages of the Windows operating system
- searching for files and folders
- using the Run option
- On-Screen Keyboard
- Control Panel – display, mouse, regional settings

## Operating System

An operating system acts as an interface between the user and the computer. It provides a software platform on which an application program runs.

Microsoft Windows is the most popular and widely used operating system. You will now learn more about Microsoft Windows. This chapter uses Windows 7. You can find Windows 10 updates at the end of the chapter.

### Advantages of the Windows operating system

Windows is an operating system which supports the Graphical User Interface environment. All commands can be executed easily and efficiently at a click of the mouse.

Some of the advantages of Windows as an operating system are listed below.

1. **Graphical User Interface**: This is also known as a GUI. It offers graphical icons and visual indicators on its interface as compared to a text-based interface called a Character User Interface (CUI).

2. **Easy to use and learn**: Working with Windows is easy as it requires just a few mouse-clicks to do the work.

3. **Multitasking**: In Windows, you can work on multiple programs at the same time. Programs open in the form of a window, which can be easily controlled with the help of the **Alt + Tab** keys. For example, you can create documents and listen to music on a computer at the same time.

*Using Alt + Tab keys to view different windows*

## Search Option

Have you ever needed to search for a file on your computer? Perhaps you wrote a letter to someone and wanted to see its content again. Maybe you saved a report on your computer and forgot its location. The **Search option** is the most convenient way to find things on your computer. The exact location of the items does not matter as the search box will search your programs and folders to find the items you are looking for.

The Search option can be found as a box in the Start menu. It is mainly used for searching files and folders stored on the computer disk. It can search for a document, an application, a computer or a user connected on the network. The search criteria can also contain text or a phrase which is a part of the document.

Follow these steps to search for a file or a folder.

1. Click on the **Start** button.

2. Type the file or folder name or keywords in the search box in the lower-left corner.

*Selecting the Search option*

3. While typing, the items matching your search text will appear in the **Start** menu. Click on your chosen file to open it.

To search for a file in a folder or library follow the steps given below.

1. Open the chosen folder or library.

2. Type the file name, or a word or a part of the word contained in the file, in the search box.

3. All the files containing the word or part of the word will be listed in the Search Results. Click on the chosen file to open it.

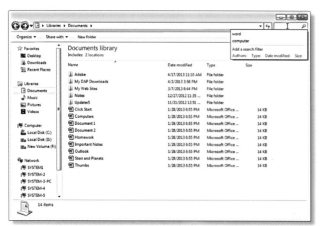

*Searching for a file in a folder*

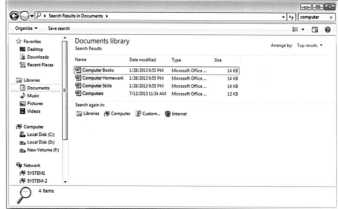

*List of files containing the typed keyword*

## ACTIVITY

Complete the following activities.

1. Do you like listening to music while working on a computer? You can open the Windows Media Player and play your favourite music. Minimise the window and continue doing your work. While performing this activity, think what feature of the Windows operating system is being used.

2. Create a music folder containing songs of your choice and then search in this folder using the Search option. Can you find the song you wish to listen to?

## Run Option

The Run option from the Start menu is used for executing a file or an application directly. For example, the user can open the Paint application by specifying **Paint** in the **Run** dialog box.

Follow the steps given below:

1. Click on **Start** ⟹ **All Programs** ⟹ **Accessories** ⟹ **Run** option
2. The **Run** dialog box opens.
3. In this dialog box, type the name of the file or program in the **Open** text box.
4. Click on **OK**.
5. If the exact location of the program or document is not known, then click the **Browse** button and select the program or document from the specified folder.

*Run dialog box*

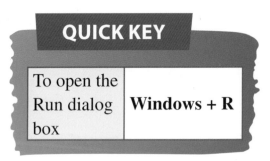

| QUICK KEY | |
|---|---|
| To open the Run dialog box | **Windows + R** |

## On-Screen Keyboard

The **On-Screen Keyboard** is an important utility program. It displays a virtual keyboard on the computer screen which allows the user to use the mouse pointer to type. The On-Screen Keyboard can also help people who do not know how to type and for whom using the mouse click is easier than using a keyboard.

Follow these steps to access the On-Screen Keyboard:

1. Click on the **Start** ⟹ **All Programs** ⟹ **Accessories** ⟹ **Ease of Access** ⟹ **On-Screen Keyboard** option.
2. The On-Screen Keyboard appears on the screen.

## ACTIVITY

A. Complete the following activity.

1. Open Paint using the Search option.

2. Create any pattern for the desktop background and write one sentence on it using the On-Screen Keyboard.

3. Save the file by the name 'MyDesktop.bmp'.

4. Close the file.

B. Think why is it safer to use the Online Virtual Keyboard while doing online banking.

## Control Panel

You can use the Control Panel to change settings for Windows. These settings control nearly everything about how Windows looks and works. You can use the Control Panel to make changes to the look and settings of Windows, including the color of your desktop, windows, hardware and software setup and configuration, network, internet, etc. You can also change the appearance of icons in the Control Panel window using the **View by** option.

View by: option

*Control Panel window*

15

The name of an application may vary with the version of an operating system. For example, in Windows XP, you see **Display**, while the same option in Windows 7 is **Personalization**.

## Personalization icon

In Windows 7, the Personalization icon of the Control Panel is used for changing the appearance of the desktop such as the background, screen saver, colors and sounds.

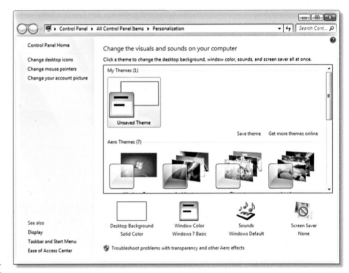

Follow these steps to change the theme of a desktop:

1. Click on **Start** ⟹ **Control Panel**.

2. In the **Control Panel** window, select the **Personalization** icon.

3. The **Personalization** window opens.

*Personalization window*

A theme is a background with a set of sounds, icons and other elements that helps you to customise your computer.

4. Click on the theme of your choice from the categories given. The computer will ask you to wait for some time showing the **Please Wait** box and then the selected theme will be applied.

5. You can further enhance your theme effects using options like selecting specific pictures, **Picture position, Change picture every**, **Shuffle** checkbox (when active) in the **Desktop Background** window.

6. You can also change the color of your window and add sound effects using the **Window Color** and **Sounds** options in the **Personalization** window.

*Selecting themes for the desktop*

## Mouse settings

You can change the mouse settings such as button configuration, double-click speed, mouse pointer shape, motion speed and trails with the help of the mouse icon.

Follow these steps to change the mouse settings for button configuration:

1. Click on **Start** ⟹ **Control Panel**.
2. In the **Control Panel** window, click on the **Mouse** icon.
3. The **Mouse Properties** window opens.
4. Click on the **Buttons** tab.
5. In the **Button configuration** section, the default use of the mouse is set for right-handed people. That is, the left button for click and double-click, and the right button for shortcut menus. But if you want to reverse the buttons, then click on the **Switch primary and secondary buttons** checkbox.

*Using Mouse Properties window*

6. You can also change the speed of double-click by dragging the pointer either to the right or left in the **Double-click speed** section.
7. Click on the **Turn on ClickLock** option in the **ClickLock** section, if you want to drag the mouse without holding down the mouse button.
8. Click on **Apply** and then click on **OK**.

Follow these steps to change the shape of the mouse pointer:

1. Click on **Start** ⟹ **Control Panel** ⟹ **Mouse** icon.
2. Click on the **Pointers** tab.
3. Select the chosen option from the predefined set of mouse pointers available on the **Scheme** drop-down list.
4. Based on the category selected, a list of mouse pointers will be displayed in the **Customize** section.

*Using the Pointer tab of Mouse Properties*

5. If you want a pointer shadow then click on the **Enable pointer shadow** checkbox.

6. Click on **Apply** and then click on **OK**.

Follow these steps to change the Pointer Options of the mouse:

1. Click on **Start** ⟹ **Control Panel** ⟹ **Mouse** icon.

2. Click on the **Pointer Options** tab.

3. Select the chosen pointer speed by dragging the pointer either to the left to slow the pointer down or to the right to make the pointer move faster in the **Motion** section.

*Pointer Options of Mouse Properties*

4. If you want the mouse pointer to point to the default button in a dialog box, then click on the **Automatically move pointer to the default button in a dialog box** checkbox in the **Snap To** section.

5. Select the **Display pointer trails** checkbox in the **Visibility** section if you want the pointer to trail the mouse on the screen.

6. If you want the mouse pointer not to be visible when you type, then click on the **Hide pointer while typing** checkbox.

7. Click on **Apply** and then click on **OK**.

## Region and Language icon

The Region and Language icon is used for changing the settings of the display of languages, numbers, time and date.

Follow the steps given below:

1. Click on **Start** ⟹ **Control Panel**.

2. In **Control Panel** window, click on the **Regional and Language** icon.

3. The **Region and Language** dialog box opens.

*Region and Language dialog box*

4. The date and time formats can be changed from the respective drop-down lists in the **Date and time formats** section.

5. Click on **Apply** and then click on **OK**.

## ACTIVITY

Complete the following activity.

1. Open the Personalization window using the Control Panel.

2. Use the file 'MyDesktop.bmp' created in the previous activity in Paint and set it as the Desktop background.

3. Change the mouse settings by increasing the double-click speed, apply the mouse trail and change the shape of the mouse pointer.

4. Change the time to the 24 hours format.

## GLOSSARY

**Desktop background**   An image used as a background on a computer screen.

**Graphical User Interface (GUI)**   An interface that uses graphical icons and visual indicators rather than text.

**Multitasking**   The ability to do more than one thing on a computer at a time.

**Theme**   A background with a set of sound, icons and other elements that helps you to customise your computer.

**Virtual keyboard**   A utility program that displays an on-screen keyboard allowing the mouse pointer to type.

1. An operating system acts as an interface between the user and the machine.

2. Windows is an operating system which supports the Graphical User Interface environment. All commands can be executed easily and efficiently with a mouse-click.

3. The Search box is located in the Start menu. It is mainly used to search for files and folders stored on a computer disk.

4. The Run option located in the Start button is used for executing a file or application directly.

5. The Control Panel allows the user to display and make changes to various basic settings of the computer system.

6. The Personalization icon located in the Control Panel is used for changing the appearance of the desktop such as the background, screen saver, colors and sounds.

7. The Mouse icon in the Control Panel is used for changing the mouse settings, such as the button configuration, double-click speed, mouse pointer shape and motion speed and trails.

8. The Region and Language icon of the Control Panel is used for changing the settings of the display of languages, numbers, time and date.

## EXERCISE

### A. True or false?

1. Personalization settings save the file from unwanted damage.

2. The On-Screen Keyboard is not an important utility program.

3. The Search option is located in the Start menu.

4. Windows is a Graphics User Interface.

5. The Run option is located on the desktop.

**B. Solve the crossword using the clues given.**

**Across**

2. The On-Screen Keyboard displays a ............... keyboard on the computer screen.

4. Alt + ............... keys are used to control open windows on the desktop.

6. The............... icon of the Control Panel is used for changing the appearance of the desktop.

7. ............... is used to change settings for windows.

**Down**

1. The ............... from the Start button is used for executing a file or application directly.

3. We use ............... to work on multiple programs for Windows.

4. ............... is a background with a set of sound, icons and other elements that helps you to customise your computer.

5. The full form of GUI is ............... User Interface.

**C. Give one word for each of the following:**

1. The option used in the Start menu to execute a file or an application directly. ...............................

2. A virtual keyboard. ...............................

3. The icon used for setting a Screen saver in the Control Panel. ...............................

4. The option used for locating the files and folders stored on a computer disk. ...............................

5. The icon used for changing the date and time settings in the Control Panel. ...............................

## D. Answer the following questions.

1. State any three advantages of using Windows as an operating system.
2. Why do you use the Run option in the Start menu?
3. What is the use of the search box in the Start menu?
4. What are the icons available in the Control Panel?
5. Discuss the usage of the Region and Language icon.

## LAB WORK

Complete the following activity.

1. Find the icons present on your desktop and make a list of them in your notebook.
2. Design a poster on Microsoft Word or Paint to describe the features of your favourite icon.
3. Change the desktop wallpaper and screen saver of your computer.
4. Before leaving the lab, reset the settings to default.

## PROJECT WORK

Open the Control Panel on your computer and explore different features. Design a presentation to provide ten tips to keep your system organised.

## WHO AM I?

I was born on 28 September 1925 in Chippewa Falls, USA. I have worked extensively on computer technologies ranging from vacuum tubes and magnetic amplifiers to transistors. I designed the first fully transistorised computers.
I also created the first supercomputer, named Cray-1 in 1976.
I am .......................................

- Windows 7 was designed for desktops and laptops but Windows 10 as an operating system is available for all devices such as PCs, laptops, mobiles, tablets and Xbox.

- The Search button on the taskbar says 'Type here to search' or 'Search the web and Windows' or 'Search Windows' depending on the version of Windows 10.

- Cortana is a personal digital assistant created by Microsoft just like Siri in Apple devices. These can set reminders, find files, search information on the internet and do many other tasks.

- The Control Panel is more organised compared to Windows 7.

- The Personalization window can be accessed in two ways:

  **Start ⟹ Control panel ⟹ Appearance and Personalization**

  Right click on **Desktop ⟹ Personalize** option

- Click on **Start ⟹ Control Panel ⟹ Clock and Region** to change Date and Time format.

# MS Office
# 3 at a Glance

## SNAP RECAP

List the various components of MS Office you have heard of.

## Introduction

Microsoft Office (MS Office) is a package provided by Microsoft Corporation which includes various application softwares used for a variety of purposes, such as MS Word for creating and processing word documents, MS Access for creating and maintaining a database, etc. The common features of all versions of MS Office are explained in this chapter. You can find MS Office 2016 updates at the end of the chapter.

### LEARNING OBJECTIVES

*You will learn about:*

- applications of MS Office
- components of the MS Office 2010 window
- creating documents using MS Word
- creating presentations using MS PowerPoint 2010 and its features
- tabular data manipulation using MS Excel

### FACT FILE

MS Office packages also come in various suites suitable for home, business, etc.

Since the first release of MS Office, several other versions have been released in the Windows platform. These are:

| | | |
|---|---|---|
| Microsoft Office 95 | Microsoft Office 97 | Microsoft Office 2000 |
| Microsoft Office 2002 (XP) | Microsoft Office 2003 | Microsoft Office 2007 |
| Microsoft Office 2010 | Microsoft Office 2013 | Microsoft Office 2016 |
| | Microsoft Office 2019 | |

Brainstorm about the different types of operating system and office packages provided by different companies and list the uses of each of them.

## Applications of Microsoft Office

Microsoft Office is designed to create a productive and efficient work environment. Each application has a similar look and feel. The skills learnt in one application can be used in other applications. Data can be easily duplicated between applications, reducing the time required to produce a new document. For example, spreadsheet data can be copied to a word processing tool without having to retype the information.

Let us learn about some of these components.

### MS Word

MS Word is a word processing application. It is used to create, edit and manage documents.

### MS PowerPoint

MS PowerPoint is a presentation application. It is used for preparation of slides with different text, graphics and animation effects.

### MS Excel

MS Excel is a spreadsheet application. It is used for calculation, analysis and visualisation of data.

### MS Access

MS Access is a database management application. It is used for creating and updating data in the form of tables.

### MS Outlook

MS Outlook is an application designed to manage your emails. It helps you to send and receive emails, manage your tasks, schedules and contacts.

## MS Publisher

MS Publisher is a desktop publishing application. It is used to create publications like office reports, brochures, business cards and newsletters.

## MS OneNote

This is a computer program in the MS Office suite that is used to create notes. It includes handwritten or typed notes that can contain tables, pictures and drawings.

# Components of the Microsoft Office 2010 Window

Each application of Microsoft Office 2010 works in the form of a window. The window is the application interface. It is made up of several components.

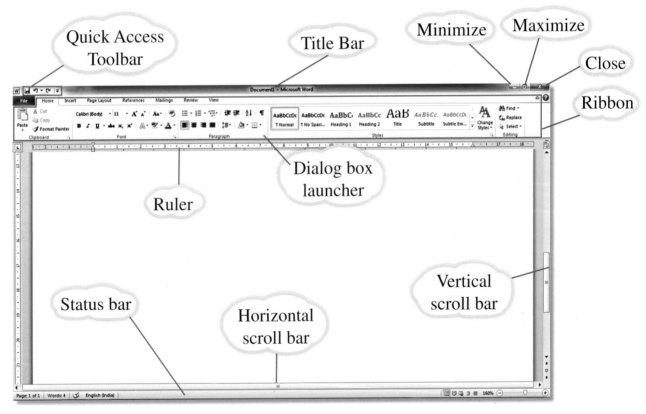

*Components of the MS Office 2010 Window*

## Title bar

The title bar displays the title of the MS Office application being used along with the default file name.

Whenever an application is opened, a file has a default name. For example, in MS Word 2010, the default file name is Document1. In MS Excel 2010, the default file name is Book1.

## Ribbon

The Ribbon is made up of **tabs**, **groups** and **commands**.

Tabs represent an activity, where each tab has groups with related activities and the commands under each group contain a menu or a box with options.

## Quick Access toolbar

This is seen above the Ribbon. It contains the most commonly repeated actions in the MS application like Undo, Redo, Save, etc. The user can customise this toolbar according their individual requirements.

## Status bar

This shows the status of the document in use. For example, in MS Word 2010, it shows the current page number along with the total pages, the word count, the language being used, the zoom level and the layout of the file.

## Horizontal scroll bar

This helps you to scroll either to the left or to the right, to see the data currently not visible on the screen.

## Vertical scroll bar

This helps you to scroll either to the top or bottom of the screen.

## Minimize button

This is the first button at the upper-right corner of the window. It displays the window in the form of a small icon on the taskbar.

## Maximize/Restore Down button

This button helps you to either display the window in full screen or in normal size.

## Close button

The last button at the upper-right corner of the screen. It helps you to close the window.

## Microsoft Word

MS Word is a word-processing tool used to create professional-looking documents. The documents can include text, graphics, table, clip art, borders, shading, etc. These documents can be created, saved, edited and printed as and when required. You have learnt about Microsoft Word in previous classes.

**ACTIVITY**

 **A.** Rahul is fond of watching biographical movies. Help him do the following:

1. Create a new word document and write a paragraph titled 'My Favourite Biographical Movie'.

2. Save it with the name – MyFile.docx.

3. Print the file to submit it to his teacher.

4. Close the file and Exit from MS Word 2010.

**QUICK KEY**

| | | | |
|---|---|---|---|
| To create a new file | **Ctrl + N** | To close a file | **Alt + F4** |
| To open an already existing file | **Ctrl + O** | To select the entire text | **Ctrl + A** |
| To save a file | **Ctrl + S** | Microsoft Word Help | **F1** |
| To print a file | **Ctrl + P** | | |

## Microsoft PowerPoint

MS PowerPoint is a powerful tool to create professional presentations and slide shows from scratch or by using the easy-to-use Wizard. It is a tool for presenting ideas and information in an interesting manner.

It allows you to place the content into a series of slides which can then be projected (using a projector) to an audience, or printed and distributed as handouts, or published online using different file formats.

## Important features of MS PowerPoint 2010

MS PowerPoint is widely used by business people, educators, students, etc. to present their ideas. Some of the important features of MS PowerPoint 2010 are discussed below.

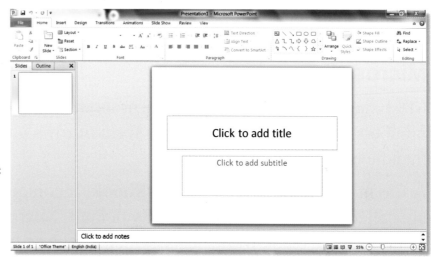

*MS PowerPoint 2010*

## Slide Layouts

These are predefined layouts for slides, which can be selected according to the user's requirements. It is important to choose a clear slide layout to make an effective presentation.

## Design Themes

These are predefined backgrounds for slides. When a suitable template is selected, then slides appear with a shaded background or a colorful pattern. You may start adding content to these slides. This is an easy way to make interesting presentations.

## Animations and Sound Effects

PowerPoint is also a multimedia application. It can be used to add text, various types of images, sound and video clips to a presentation.

### QUICK KEY

| | |
|---|---|
| To cut any data in a slide | Ctrl + X |
| To copy any data from a slide | Ctrl + C |
| To paste data anywhere in a slide | Ctrl + V |

Prepare a PowerPoint presentation on the components of MS Office, their respective features and use. Save your presentation and then exit from MS PowerPoint.

## Microsoft Excel

MS Excel is a popular spreadsheet program that allows you to work with numbers. You can store data in the form of rows and columns which can then be organised and processed.

A file in MS Excel is called a **workbook**. It contains many pages which are called **worksheets** or **sheets**. By default, Microsoft Excel workbook contains three blank worksheets, which are identified by tabs displayed at the bottom of the document.

Each sheet is divided into a grid of rows and columns. The columns are named as A, B, C,... Z, AA, AB, AC and so on, and there are 16,384 such combinations. The rows are numbered from 1 to 1,048,576. The number of columns and rows in a worksheet depends on the memory of the computer and the system resources.

The intersection of a row and a column is called a **cell**. Each cell is referred by an address called the **cell address**. For example, B12, A3, G5, etc.

Any cell which is selected is an **active cell**.

All the basic components of a MS Office window are listed here.

1. **Formula Bar**: This bar is found below the Ribbon. It contains the formula entered in a cell. The formula in Excel should begin with an equal to (=) sign.
2. **Name Box**: This contains the cell address of the active cell.
3. **Sheet Tabs**: These tabs are found below the workbook in the lower left corner. These tabs help us to select different worksheets in a workbook.

MS Excel can be used for calculation, database management, preparation of charts, etc. These are discussed here.

## Calculation

You can do any kind of calculation using formulae and functions. These formulae can be easily copied and managed. If you make any changes in the functions and formulae within the spreadsheet, the computer automatically re-calculates the final values.

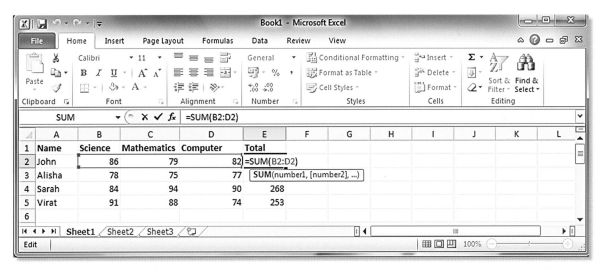

*Calculation in MS Excel*

## Database management

This feature is extremely important when dealing with a large amount of data, which could be a few hundred or even thousands of records. For example, if a teacher wishes to record all the details of the students in their class along with their marks, it can be easily managed using this feature. It helps us to create, edit, sort and filter data according to our needs.

## Charts

These are a pictorial representation of data. You can create different types of graph easily from the data in the spreadsheet. Charts, once created, can be easily changed in terms of the chart text, color, size, position, etc.

**TRY THIS**

MS Office components have similar steps and shortcut keys to create, open, save, close and print files. Open the files from different applications and try the shortcuts.

Prepare an Excel sheet to calculate the average temperature of the last ten days. Use a chart to show the rise and fall in temperature.

**GLOSSARY**

**Database management**   The process of managing a large amount of information stored on a computer.

**MS Access**   A database management application.

**MS Excel**   A spreadsheet application to work well with numbers.

**MS Office**   A collection of software of Windows-based applications.

**MS OneNote**   A computer program part of Microsoft Office suite and is used to create notes.

**MS Outlook**   An application designed to manage your emails.

**MS PowerPoint**   An application to create presentations and slide shows.

**MS Publisher**   A desktop publishing application.

**MS Word**   A word-processing tool to create professional documents.

**Spreadsheet**   A computer program that helps you to do calculations and planning.

**YOU ARE HERE**

**3**

1. Applications in the MS Office suite include MS Word, MS Excel, MS PowerPoint, MS Access, MS Outlook, MS OneNote and MS Publisher.

2. MS Word can include text, graphics, tables, Clip Art, borders, shading, etc. These documents may be created, saved, edited and printed as and when required.

3. MS PowerPoint is one of the most powerful tools for communicating ideas and information in the form of slide shows.

4. You can store data in MS Excel in the form of rows and columns that can then be organised and processed.

# EXERCISE

## A. Fill in the blanks.

1. .................................... is designed to create a productive and efficient work environment.
2. The Ribbon includes tabs, groups and ........................ .
3. Microsoft Word is a tool which is used to create professional-looking ........................... .
4. ............................. . can be used for calculation, database management and preparation of charts.
5. ............................. is a pictorial representation of data.

## B. True or false?

1. In MS Word, the default file name is Document1 and in MS Excel the default file name is Book1.

2. The user cannot customise the Quick Access toolbar according to their individual requirements.

3. A file in MS Excel is called a worksheet.

4. MS PowerPoint is a multimedia application.

5. Spreadsheet is a computer program that helps you to do drawing only.

## C. Write the shortcut keys for the following.

1. To open an already existing file  .................................

2. Microsoft Word Help  .................................

3. To select the entire text  .................................

4. To print a file  .................................

5. To cut any data from an MS PowerPoint slide  .................................

**D.  Match the following.**

1.  MS Word                   a.  Desktop publishing application

2.  MS PowerPoint         b.  Database management

3.  MS Excel                c.  Presentation application

4.  MS Publisher          d.  Spreadsheet application

5.  MS Access             e.  Word-processing application

**E.  Answer the following questions.**

1.  List the different components of MS Office.
2.  What is MS Word used for?
3.  Write down the steps for adding transitions to a slide.
4.  Explain any three important features of MS Excel.
5.  List the components that are common in the windows of all the applications of MS Office.

**LAB WORK**

A.  In MS Word, create a report titled 'My Favourite IT personality'.

B.  A science teacher wants to explain the topic 'the Solar System' through a presentation. Suggest an MS Office application that they can use for this purpose.

C.  Rita wants to make a chart to make a comparison of the storybooks among her friends. Suggest a suitable MS Office application to use. Write a few important characteristics of the application.

D.  In MS Excel, create a shopping list with the following columns: name, quantity, price per item and amount spent per item. Add at least eight shopping items.

E.  Besides MS Word, MS Excel and MS PowerPoint, there are a few other applications offered by MS Office 2010. Make a presentation on these with a brief explanation about each of them.

## PROJECT WORK

Create a presentation on any version of MS Office and share the link of the presentation with your friends to gain insight about various versions of MS Office.

**Office 2016 Updates**

- Microsoft Office 2016 introduces a colorful theme where each application has a different color. For example, MS Word is given dark blue, MS Excel is green, MS PowerPoint is orange, etc. However, we can change this default theme color by selecting **File ⟹ Account ⟹ Office Theme**. The options available for changing theme are colorful dark grey and white.

- MS Office 2016 has a bulb icon '**Tell me what you want to do**' just above the ribbon. It helps you to look for any information in the software.

- Files created in MS Office 2016 can be shared with others for either editing or viewing. Select **File ⟹ Share** option to upload a file to your cloud so that it can be shared with other people.

- MS Word 2016 has an improved grammar checker; MS Excel 2016 has added a few new charts.

# MS Word 2010 —
# Inserting Objects and Drawing

## SNAP RECAP

1. Name the alignments available in MS Word 2010.
2. Name any four formatting tools available on the Home tab of MS Word 2010.

## LEARNING OBJECTIVES

*You will learn about:*

- inserting pictures, Clip Art and WordArt
- inserting page numbers

## Introduction

MS Word 2010 allows you to insert objects in a document, such as a picture, Clip Art and WordArt. These objects can be resized, copied, moved and cropped easily. Documents can be improved by using suitable tools. This chapter uses MS Word 2010. You will find updates for MS Word 2016 at the end of the chapter.

## FACT FILE

MS Word allows you to protect a document. This restricts others from viewing and editing it. You may also select parts of a document that need to be protected.

## Inserting Pictures

A document can be made more attractive with pictures or photos. This can be done using the following steps.

1. Click on **Insert** tab ⟹ **Illustrations** group ⟹ **Picture** option.

*Inserting a picture in an MS Word 2010 document*

2. An **Insert Picture** dialog box appears. Here, you may browse or type the location (or path) of the picture on the computer.

3. Select the chosen picture and then click on the **Insert** button.

Complete the following activity.

1. Save pictures of your group of friends in a folder.

2. Open a new document. Write about your friends.

3. Insert the pictures in this document.

4. Save it with the name OurGroupRocks.docx.

## Inserting Clip Art

Clip Art is a picture or a graphic image that can be inserted into an MS Word document. Clip Art comes in a wide variety of formats and styles, from a simple cartoon to a photographic image.

Microsoft Word comes with its own Clip Art collection that you can use. The steps to insert a Clip Art item are:

1. Open a new document or click on the location in the document where you wish to insert a Clip Art.

2. Click on **Insert** tab ⟹ **Illustrations** group ⟹ **Clip Art** option.

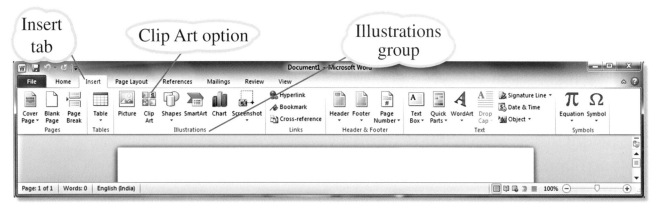

*Insert Clip Art*

3. The **Clip Art** task pane appears on the right side of the window.

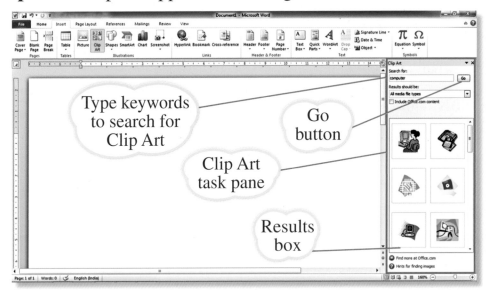

*Clip Art task pane*

4. Type the keywords that describe the Clip Art you want in the **Search for** field.

To narrow down the search, you may click on the drop-down arrows in the **Results should be** fields. Then select the appropriate options.

5. Click on the **Go** button.

6. Move the mouse pointer to the image of your choice in the result box. Right click on that image and select **Insert**.

7. The image will be inserted at the selected location.

Type only meaningful words in the **Search for** field and then click on the **Go** button.

## Steps for resizing a Clip Art

The Clip Art pictures can be resized, rotated or cropped (to cut from the edges) depending on the requirement. The steps for resizing Clip Art are given below.

1. Select the picture. When the picture is selected it is surrounded by a border with resizing handles.

**TRY THIS**

When you select a picture, the **Format** tab opens automatically. Select the ⬐▾ tool to rotate or the ⬚ tool to crop the Clip Art picture.

2. Move the mouse pointer over one of the little resizing handles.

3. The shape of the mouse pointer will change to a double-headed arrow.

4. When the pointer has changed its shape, hold the left mouse button.

5. With the left mouse button held down, drag the mouse until the picture is the size you want.

**ACTIVITY**

Complete the activity.

1. Write about some historic places in a Word document.

2. Search for some relevant pictures in the Clip Art gallery on your computer.

3. Add those pictures to your document.

## Inserting WordArt

WordArt is a predefined text format with a well-defined font size, style and color. This can be added to your document. Let us explore it in this section.

The steps to insert WordArt are:

1. Select **Insert** tab ⟹ **Text** group ⟹ **WordArt** option.

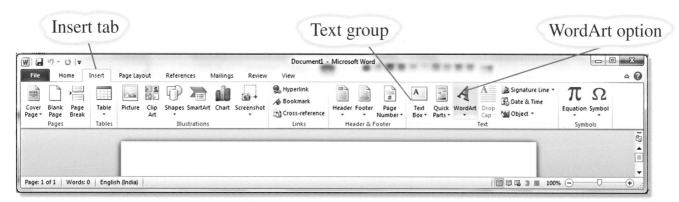

*Inserting WordArt*

2. Click on the **WordArt** drop-down list.

3. As you can see, there are lots of different styles to choose from. Select a style by clicking on it with the left mouse button.

WordArt drop-down list

*WordArt drop-down list*

4. The edited WordArt text will appear in the document and you will see that the **Format** tab appears.

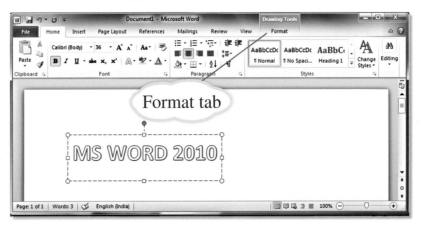

*Format tab in MS Word 2010*

5. Click various options in the different groups of the **Format** tab and see what it does to your WordArt. You can do things like change the letter spacing, edit text, add a different color, add 3-D and shadow effects and rotate the text.

**ACTIVITY**

Complete the following activity.

1. In the document OurGroupRocks.docx that you created in the previous activity, add a heading using WordArt.

2. Try using WordArt in different styles at suitable places in the document.

3. Save the changes in your document.

Click anywhere on the document. Press the **Alt** key and observe the Ribbon.

Press **Alt** + the letter highlighted below the Ribbon component of your choice to open that component. For example, press **Alt + N** to open the **Insert** tab.

## GLOSSARY

**Clip Art**  A picture or a graphic image that can be inserted into an MS Word document.

**Graphic**  The design of pictures or text for books, magazines, advertisements, etc.

**WordArt**  A predefined text format with a specific font size.

**YOU ARE HERE**

**4**

1. A Word document can be made more attractive with pictures or photographs. This can be done by clicking on Insert tab ⟹ Illustrations group ⟹ Picture option.

2. Clip Art is available in a wide variety of formats and styles, from a simple cartoon to a photographic image.

3. Clip Art can be inserted by clicking on Insert tab ⟹ Illustrations group ⟹ Clip Art option.

4. To add a WordArt, click on Insert tab ⟹ Text group ⟹ WordArt drop-down list.

5. Microsoft Word allows you to insert page numbers into your document. To insert page numbers, click on Insert tab ⟹ Header & Footer group ⟹ Page Numbers drop-down list.

6. The Shapes drop-down list is used to insert and format the objects in a MS Word 2010 document.

## EXERCISE

**A. Fill in the blanks.**

1. ........................ is the design of pictures or text for books, magazines, advertisements, etc.

2. ........................ is a picture or a graphic image that can be inserted into an MS Word document.

3. The ................. is a predefined text format with a well-defined font size, style and color.

4. ........................ is a shortcut key for inserting page numbers in a document.

**B. Name the following tools and then write their function.**

| Icon | Name | Function |
|---|---|---|
| ✏️ | | |
| 𝐴 WordArt | | |
| ⇨⇦⇧⇩⇲⇱✦⚓⛳⌂⛶⛶ ⌯⌡⌢⌣⇨⇨▭❯⛳⛶⛶⛶ ⛶⛶⌢ | | |
| Clip Art | | |
| ▢ | | |

**C. Find the error and write the corrected statement in your notebook.**

1. To add WordArt, click on the Insert tab ⟹ Text group ⟹ Drop-down list.

2. To insert page numbers, click on the Insert tab ⟹ Page group ⟹ Page Numbers drop-down list.

3. Clip Art can be inserted by clicking on the Design tab ⟹ Illustrations group ⟹ Clip Art option.

4. Inserting pictures/photographs can be done by clicking on the Layout tab ⟹ Header & Footer group ⟹ Picture option.

## D. Answer the following questions.

1. How do you insert pictures in a document?
2. What is Clip Art?
3. Give the steps to insert page numbers in a document.
4. What is the purpose of the Shapes drop-down list?
5. Explain any two features for formatting WordArt.
6. The Clip Art picture can be resized, rotated or cropped. State how.

## LAB WORK

A. In MS Word, create your own story with illustrations.
   1. Insert pictures and Clip Art at appropriate places.
   2. Give the story a title and insert page numbers at the bottom of each page.
   3. You can also create your own pictures using Shapes.
   4. Apply formatting features to the text.
B. Imagine that you are assigned the duty of being an editor of the school magazine. Create a report on the 'Annual Sports Day Celebration' in the school.
C. Write a short poem on a topic of your choice and insert suitable pictures and Clip Art.

## PROJECT WORK

Design a birthday card for the birthday of a family member or friend. Insert pictures and headings using the Word Art feature of Microsoft Word 2010.

- The **Illustrations** group of MS Word 2016 is slightly different from that of MS Word 2010.

*MS Word 2016*

*MS Word 2010*

- In MS Word 2016, you can insert pictures From File and Online.

  **Insert ⟹ Illustrations** group ⟹ **Pictures** (to insert pictures **From File**)

  **Insert ⟹ Illustrations** group ⟹ **Online Pictures** (to insert pictures from internet)

- You can use the **Online Pictures** option for inserting Clip Art. The steps for finding and inserting clip art are given below:

  1. Select **Insert** tab ⟹ **Illustrations** group ⟹ **Online Pictures**. A pop-up will appear allowing you to search Office.com or Bing.

  2. In one of the search boxes, type a keyword for the Clip Art you would like to find. For example, if you type 'computer' you will get related images.

  3. From the list of pictures displayed, select the picture(s) you would like to add then click the **Insert** button.

# MS PowerPoint 2010 – Editing and Formatting Slides

5

## Introduction

**Editing** refers to making changes in a document by modifying, arranging and tracking, etc. **Formatting** means to change the layout of the document through enhancing the font style, size, themes, etc. to make the document look more presentable. This chapter uses MS PowerPoint 2010. You can find MS PowerPoint 2016 updates at the end of the chapter.

## LEARNING OBJECTIVES

*You will learn about:*

- editing a slide in MS PowerPoint 2010
- formatting a slide in MS PowerPoint 2010
- text alignment
- bullets and numbering
- changing the Theme and Background of a slide
- adding graphics to a presentation
- rearranging slides in a presentation
- slide transitions
- setting up a slideshow

*A PowerPoint slide*

# How to Edit a Slide

Editing a slide involves moving and duplicating the text.

## How to move the text

Moving the text means to 'cut' the selected text from one location of a slide and 'paste' it in another location in the same slide or another slide.

1. Select the text/object to be moved.
2. Click on the **Home** tab ⟹ **Clipboard** group ⟹ **Cut** option.
3. Place the cursor at the point where the text is to be inserted.
4. Click on the **Home** tab ⟹ **Clipboard** group ⟹ **Paste** option.

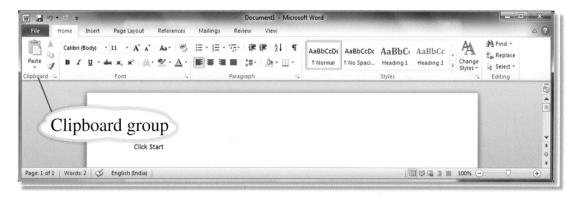

*Cut and Paste options*

## How to duplicate the text

Duplicating the text means 'copying' the selected text from one location and 'pasting' it in another location.

1. Select the text/object to be moved.
2. Click on the **Home** tab ⟹ **Clipboard** group ⟹ **Copy** option.
3. Place the cursor at the point where the text is to be inserted.
4. Click on the **Home** tab ⟹ **Clipboard** group ⟹ **Paste** option.

---

**FACT FILE**

Cut or copied text is placed on the Clipboard which is a temporary buffer area in the memory. The text on the **Clipboard** remains as it is, until the next **Cut** or **Copy** command is given. The **Paste** command places the last copied or cut text.

# How to Format a Slide

Format means to arrange the text according to a chosen pattern. Font, font size and style are used to define a character's format. Formatting the slides makes the presentation more effective and readable. Let us study in detail the different formatting features available.

## Font

Font refers to the shape of the text as it appears on the screen. A few examples are:

This is Myriad Pro Regular font. This is **Helvetica LT Std Black** font.

This is **ITC Bookman Std Medium** font.

## Font size

This refers to the size of the text as it appears on the screen. A few examples are:

8　　12　　20　　24　　32

## Font style

There are various styles available like **BOLD**, *Italics* and <u>Underline</u>. These are used to give an impact to the text in the presentation. The various font styles available are shown below.

*Font Styles*

| Style | Description |
|---|---|
| **Bold** | Text is printed darker so that words and phrases stand out on a page. It is often used for titles and headings. |
| *Italic* | Text is slanted and is mostly used for emphasis. It is sometimes used for headings, for highlighting scientific names, etc. |
| <u>Underline</u> | Text has a line under it. It is mostly used for emphasis. It is sometimes used for the title of a slide. |
| Superscript | Reduces the size of the text and raises it to the top of the current line. For example, $X^2$ where 2 is a superscript. |
| Subscript | Reduces the size of the text and lowers it to the bottom of the current line. For example, $H_2SO_4$ and $Log_{10} X$ where 2, 4 and 10 are subscripts. |

Regular text, sometimes called Normal text, is the default style.

## Font color

Font color can be used to improve the look of a presentation. It can also give emphasis to headings and subheadings. The example below highlights the impact of text color.

When **red** and **blue** are mixed, we get **violet**.

You can change the font, size, style and color using the **Font** group in the **Home** tab or the **Font** dialog box.

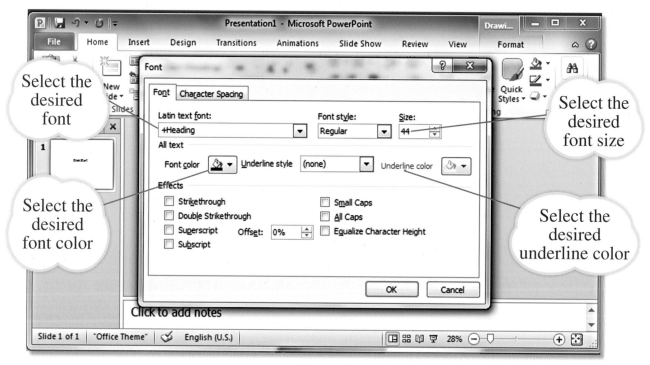

*Font dialog box*

## Format Painter

This is a special command that allows the user to copy the text format, and not the text, from one part of the text to another. All formats like font, size, font color can be copied easily using Format Painter.

The steps to use Format Painter are:

1. Select the text from where the format is to be copied.

2. Click on the **Format Painter** option in the **Clipboard** group of the **Home** tab. The mouse pointer changes to a brush.

3. Now select the text on which the format is to be applied and release the left mouse button.

52

3. The **Format Background** dialog box appears.

4. Click on the **Color** drop-down list and select the color you wish to apply to the slide's background. Click on **More Colors** to choose from a wider selection of colors.

5. When finished, click on the button that suits your need.

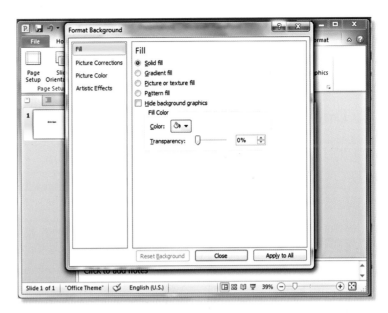

*Format Background dialog box*

| | |
|---|---|
| Reset Background | Cancels the formatted background. |
| Close | Closes the dialog box. |
| Apply to All | Applies the formatted background to all the slides. |

## How to Add Graphics to a Presentation

Graphics can be used to make a presentation more interesting. Depending on the topic, sometimes graphics can be more informative than words. Graphics in a digital format are available from various sources such as scanned images, digital camera photographs and illustration software.

### How to insert a picture

1. Click on the **Insert** tab ⟹ **Images** group ⟹ **Picture** option.

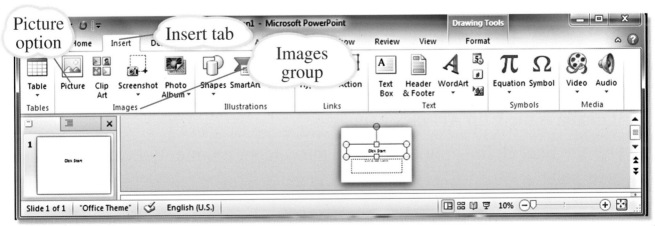

*Inserting a picture in a presentation*

2. It displays the **Insert Picture** dialog box with a list of graphic files.

3. Select the picture file most suitable for your presentation from the appropriate location. Click on the **Insert** button.

4. Drag the image using the left mouse button and click it to drop it at the chosen location on the slide.

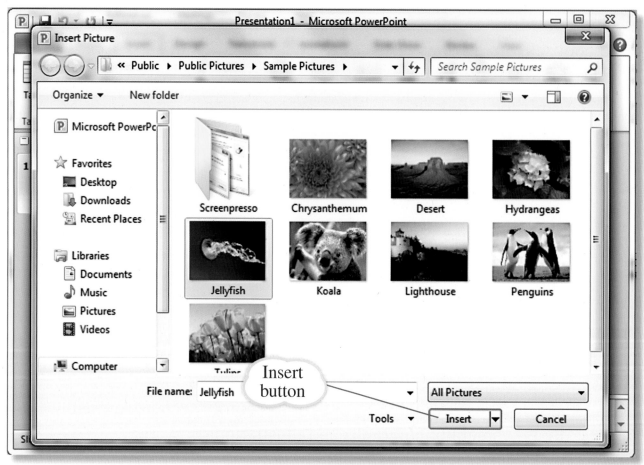

*Insert Picture dialog box*

## How to Insert Clip Art

Clip Art are files of general purpose graphics consisting of animations and cartoons.

1. Click on the **Insert** tab ⟹ **Images** group ⟹ **Clip Art** option.

2. It displays the **Clip Art** task pane.

3. Use the **Search for** option and type the category name. For example, type 'computer'.

*Inserting Clip Art*

4. Click on the **Go** button. A list of pictures in the computer category will be displayed.

5. Select the picture and click on the drop-down arrow on the right side.

6. Select **Insert** from the drop-down list.

7. The Clip Art will be inserted in the current slide. You can drag the image using the left mouse button to place it in the chosen location on the slide.

**TRY THIS**

You already have a collection of slide layouts with picture(s) in the **Office Theme** drop-down list. Use them to insert pictures and Clip Art into slides.

## How to Use SmartArt

SmartArt is a special feature of MS PowerPoint 2010 that allows the user to add graphics to the presentation grouped under different categories. It is the visual representation of text/data in the form of charts rather than tables and numbers.

Follow these steps to add SmartArt to a slide of the presentation.

1. Click on **Insert** tab ⟹ **Illustrations** group ⟹ **SmartArt** option.
2. It displays the **Choose a SmartArt Graphic** dialog box.
3. Select the category from the left pane and browse through the different SmartArt options available in the middle pane. The right pane gives a preview of the SmartArt selected.
4. Click the **OK** button to insert the selected SmartArt design and enter the appropriate text.

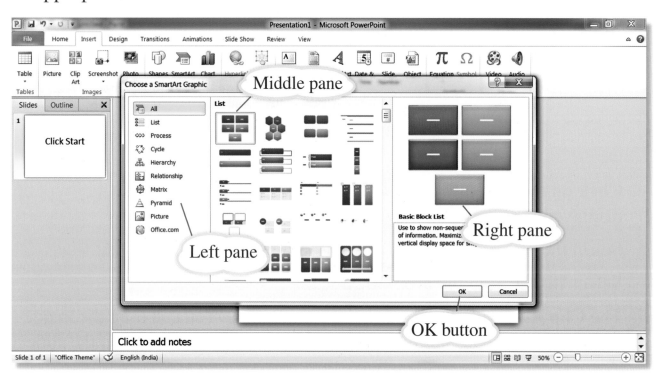

*Choosing a SmartArt Graphic dialog box*

On choosing a SmartArt design, two new tabs open up in the **Ribbon** under the **SmartArt Tools**–the **Format** tab and the **Design** tab. The different groups on these tabs can be used to edit SmartArt designs and make them suitable for the information in the slide.

## Inserting Audio and Video Files

Follow these steps to add an audio file or a video clip to the presentation.

1. Select the slide where the audio or video file has to be inserted.

2. Click on **Insert** tab ⟹ **Media** group ⟹ Video/Audio drop-down list.

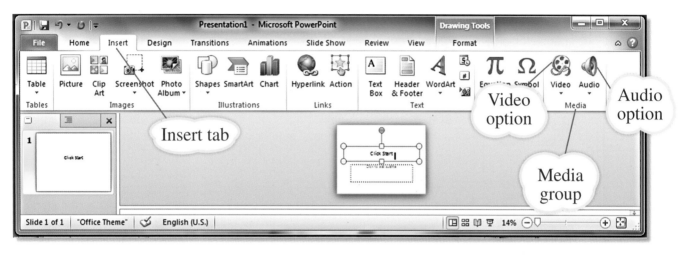

*Inserting audio and video files*

3. Click on the **Audio from File** option from the **Audio** drop-down list to insert an audio file. The **Insert** Audio/Video dialog box appears. Select the file and click on the **OK** button.

- The **Clip Art Audio** option allows the user to pick an audio file from the **Clip Art** task pane.

- Audio recordings can be done using the **Record Audio** option and can then be inserted in the slide.

*Insert Audio dialog box*

4. Click on the **Video from File** option from the drop-down list to insert a video clip into your slide. The **Insert Video** dialog box appears. Select the chosen file and click on **OK**.

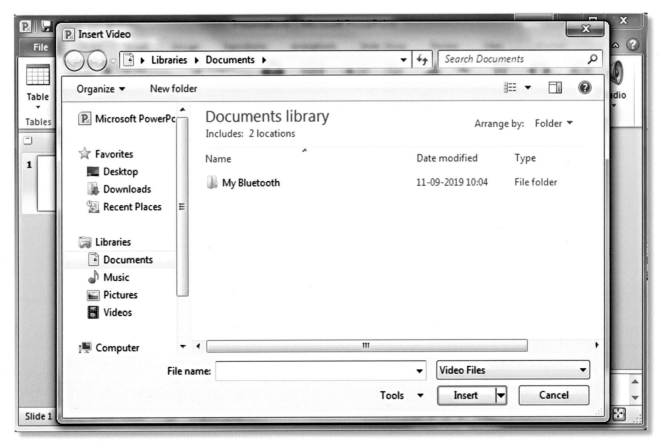

*Insert Video dialog box*

A video selected using the **Clip Art Video** option plays automatically on running the slide show.

5. When audio files are inserted, a sound icon appears on the slide.

6. On inserting an audio or a video file, an additional **Options** tab appears in the Ribbon. Options in the different groups of this tab can be used to make it suitable for the presentation.

**TRY THIS**

Try adding a video file from the Clip Organiser.

Complete the following activity.

1.  Open the presentation 'TheBigLizards.pptx' from the previous activity.
2.  Left align the text of the index slide.
3.  Align the rest of the slides as 'Justify'.
4.  Use a different color and style for the background of each section.
5.  Search for some pictures on the internet and place them on the slides or use Clip Art in appropriate parts of the presentation.
6.  Save the changes.

## How to Order Slides in a Presentation

The order of the slides can be changed easily. There are two ways to do this, which are explained here.

### Changing order in Normal view

1. Open your presentation in Normal view.

2. Select the slide that you want to move on the **Slides** tab on the left side.

3. Drag it either up or down and release it at the chosen location.

4. View your presentation to check the new order of the slides.

### Changing order in Slide Sorter view

1. Open your presentation in the **Slide Sorter** view (**View** tab ⟹ **Presentation Views** ⟹ **Slide Sorter** view).

2. Select the thumbnail of the slide of which the order is to be changed.

3. Drag it either left or right and release it at the chosen location.

4. View your presentation to check the new order of the slides.

## Slide Transition

A slide transition is the visual effect that occurs when you move from one slide to the next during a presentation. You can control the following features when a slide appears on the screen during the presentation.

1. You can move to the next slide either automatically depending on the preset timings or with the help of the mouse click.

2. You can make the slide appear on the screen following a chosen pattern like Box In, Checkerboard and Across.

3. You can add sound effects by inserting appropriate audio files.

4. You can move from one slide to the next at a specified speed.

All these features can be controlled by using the **Animations** tab. Let us follow these steps to apply a transition to a slide.

1. Select either the **Slide Sorter View** or the **Normal View** in the **Status bar**.

2. Select the **Transitions** tab.

3. From the **Transitions** tab, explore the following:

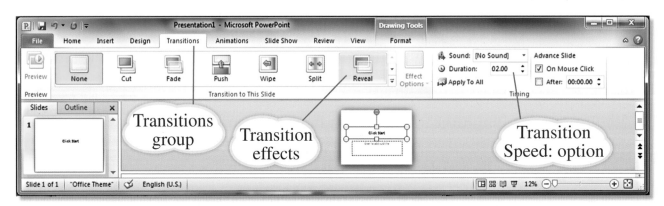

*Applying transitions to a slide*

a. Select any style from the **Transition to This Slide** group drop-down list.

b. Use the **Transition Sound** option to add sound to the slide, to be heard during the slide show.

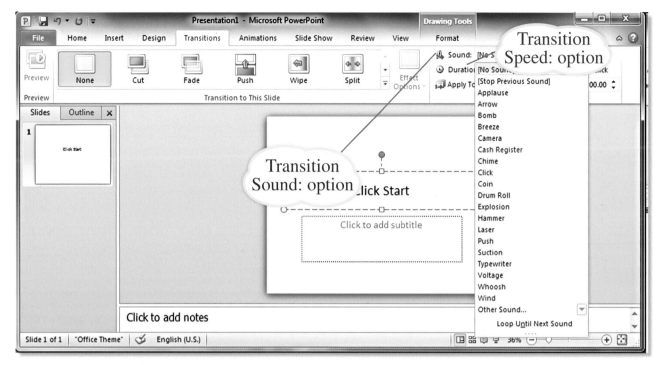

*Adding a Transition Sound to the slide*

c. Use the **Duration** option to control the speed of the transition from one slide to the next during the slide show.

d. Use the **Advance Slide** option to choose the slide transition **On Mouse Click** or **Automatically Afterwith** the specified number of seconds.

e. A transition can be applied to the current slide or to all the slides. For applying the selected transition to all the slides, click **Apply To All**.

f. For a preview of the transition applied to the current slide, click on the **Preview** option in the **Preview** group of the **Animations** tab.

4. In the **Slide Show** tab, select **From Beginning** from the **Start Slide Show** group to view the slide show from the first slide of the presentation.

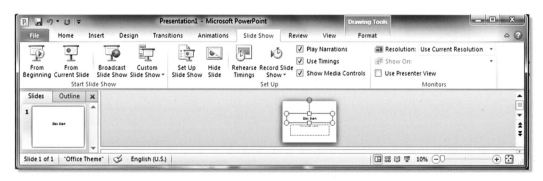

*Slide Show tab*

# Slide Show

Once you have finished creating the presentation slides, what is the next step? Yes, you guessed right! It is the PowerPoint slide show. In the slide show mode, the slides run in full screen mode. That is the actual screen that the audience will see.

There are different ways of running a slide show.

### Slide show from the first slide

Click on the **View** tab ⟹ **Presentation Views** group ⟹ **Slide Show** option.

### Slide show from the current slide

Click the **Slide Show** icon in the **Status Bar** of the PowerPoint screen.

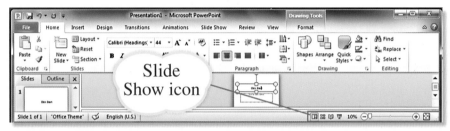

*Using the Slide Show icon in the MS PowerPoint 2010 screen*

## QUICK KEY

| To start a slide show from the first slide | **F5** |
| --- | --- |
| To start a slide show from the current slide | **Shift + F5** |

### Setting up a slide show

You can set up a slide show by using the **Set Up Show** dialog box.

1. Click on the **Slide Show** tab ⟹ **Set Up** group ⟹ **Set Up Slide Show** option. The **Set Up Show** dialog box opens.

2. In the **Show type** section, select the chosen option.

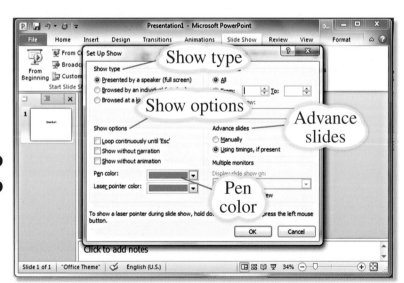

*Set Up Show dialog box*

3. In the **Show options** section, select the chosen option.
For example, **Loop continuously until 'Esc'** will help you to run the presentation continuously–that is, if the last slide of the show is shown then the slide show begins again automatically from the first slide. This will keep on repeating continuously until you press an **Escape** key.

4. In the **Advance slides** section, select the **Manually** option if slides are to be shown using the keyboard or mouse. Select the **Using timings, if present** option if the slide timings are set.

5. Select the chosen pen color from the **Pen color** drop-down list if you wish to change the mouse pointer to a pencil during a slide show.

6. Click on the **OK** button.

**ACTIVITY**

Complete the following activity.
1. Open the presentation on 'TheBigLizards.pptx' from the earlier activity in the Slide Sorter View.
2. Add transitions to the slides.
3. Let the slides advance automatically after every fifteen seconds.
4. Add sound using the audio files available on the computer system.
5. Save the changes.
6. Set up the slide show and view your presentation.

**GLOSSARY**

**Align Text Left**   Text is aligned from the left edge and is ragged from the right edge.

**Align Text Right**   Text is aligned from the right edge and is ragged from the left edge.

**Center alignment**   Aligns the text centrally and leaves the text ragged at the right and left edges.

**Format**  Arranges text according to a chosen pattern.

**Format Painter**  Allows the user to copy the text format and not the text.

**Justify alignment**  Text is aligned both left and right.

**Slide Show mode**  This option allows you to run your PowerPoint slides in full screen mode, with all the animations and transitions you selected.

**Slide transition**  Moving from one slide to another during a presentation.

**Subscript**  Reduces the size of the text and lowers it to the bottom of the current line.

**Superscript**  Reduces the size of the text and raises it to the top of the current line.

**Text alignment**  The text layout within a paragraph with respect to document margins.

**Underline style**  The font style where the text has a line under it.

**YOU ARE HERE**

**5**

1. Formatting and editing of the slides helps to make your presentation more appealing to the audience.

2. Editing a slide involves moving and duplicating text.

3. There are four types of text alignment – Right, Left, Center and Justified.

4. Sometimes you need to write information in the form of lists. These lists can be either in the form of bullets or numbers.

5. Slide Background helps you to change the background color, texture and pattern of the slides in the presentation.

6. Graphics can be used to make a presentation more interesting. They can be inserted into the slides in the form of pictures and Clip Art.

7. The order of the slides can be changed easily. Slides can be rearranged either in the Normal View or the Slide Sorter View.

## EXERCISE

**A. Fill in the blanks.**

1. Duplicating the text means ................... the selected text from one location and ............... it in another location.

2. ................... means to arrange the text according to a chosen pattern.

3. A ............... is a template with a specific design that can be applied to a slide or to the entire presentation.

4. ............... in a digital format are available from various sources such as scanned images, digital camera photographs and illustration software.

5. Clip Art are files of general purpose graphics consisting of ............. and ...................

**B. Give one word for the following.**

1. A feature of MS PowerPoint 2010 which allows the user to arrange audio and video clips on the computer.

2. A feature of MS PowerPoint 2010 which allows the user to add graphics to the presentation grouped under different categories.

3. The way in which slides appear one after the other in a slide show.

4. The alignment where the text is flushed both left and right.

**C. Match the following.**

| | | | |
|---|---|---|---|
| 1. | Copying text | a. | Ctrl + L |
| 2. | Align text left | b. | Ctrl + I |
| 3. | Italics | c. | Ctrl + A |
| 4. | Select all | d. | Ctrl + V |
| 5. | Paste | e. | Ctrl + C |

**D.  Explain the difference between:**

1.  Superscript and Subscript
2.  Cut, Paste and Copy, Paste options
3.  Bold and Italics
4.  Left and Right alignments
5.  Adding bullets and adding numbers to a list

**E.   Answer the following questions.**

1.  What is meant by a slide transition?
2.  What is meant by 'moving' and 'copying' a slide?
3.  What is meant by text alignment? Explain the different types.
4.  Write the steps to use Format Painter.
5.  How can you add graphics to a presentation?
6.  Give a one-step solution to copy the text format, and not the text, from one selection of the text to another.

**LAB WORK**

A.  Create a presentation on The Seven Wonders of the World.
B.  Create a presentation on parts of a plant.
C.  Prepare a presentation on your school. Format slides with slide transitions of your choice. The presentation should focus on the following points.

- Brief introduction about your school
- The buildings of your school
- Educational and other achievements
- Sports facilities
- Any other important information

**PROJECT WORK**

Make a presentation on the topic of national festivals. The presentation should include all the features covered in the chapter.

- A separate image group is available to manage images which can be inserted from a variety of online sources. You can use this option to insert Clip Art.

Select **Insert** tab ⟹ **Images** group ⟹ **Online Pictures**

- MS PowerPoint 2016 has new themes which you can change by selecting
**File** ⟹ **Account** ⟹ **Office Theme**.

- Draw a shape on a slide and you will see an increased number of 'preset' styles related to color and formatting options by clicking on the image under **Shape Styles** group. This makes it quicker and easier to design a presentation in MS PowerPoint 2016.

71

# Introduction to MS Excel 2010

## Introduction

MS Excel is a spreadsheet package. It is used for storing data in the form of rows and columns. It uses the concept of displaying data in the form of tables. This data can also be represented as charts and graphs. This chapter will use MS Excel 2010. You can find updates for MS Excel 2016 at the end of this chapter.

Some of the main advantages of using Excel are listed below.

1. **Calculation**: Numbers and calculations are managed efficiently in MS Excel. Once written, a formula can be easily copied to the rest of the worksheet. If any changes are made in the values, the new calculation is done automatically.

2. **Database management**: Data is a collection of values in the form of rows and columns. The data can be easily created, sorted, searched and maintained in MS Excel 2010.

**FACT FILE**

You can also insert an existing database into MS Excel.

The formula may consist of:

1. only values—for example, =5+7
2. a combination of a number and a cell address—for example, =A1+3
3. only cell addresses—for example, =D2+E2

**ACTIVITY**

Complete the following activity.
1. Create a list of car models made by different companies available in the market.
2. The list should have columns for Car name, Company name, Model number, Cost on road, Discount (20 percent) and Amount after discount.
3. Store the details of at least five cars.

## Cell Alignment

Cells can contain text, numbers, or mathematical formulae. By default:

1. text entries are left aligned.
2. numbers are right aligned.
3. formulas begin with '=' sign. These are left aligned before the Enter key is pressed. After pressing the Enter key, it gives the answer in numbers which are right aligned or text which is left aligned.

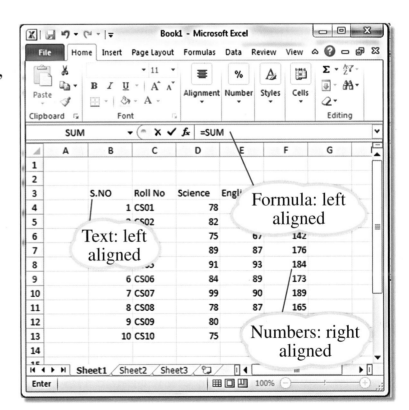

*Cell alignment*

# Inserting Rows and Columns

In a worksheet you can edit rows, columns and cells. The height of rows and the width of columns can be easily adjusted depending on your need.

## How to insert rows

1.  Select the **row label** before which a new row is to be inserted.
2.  Click on the **Home** tab.
3.  In the **Cells** group, click on the **Insert** drop-down list.
4.  From the drop-down list, select the **Insert Sheet Rows** option.
5.  A new row will be inserted above the selected row.

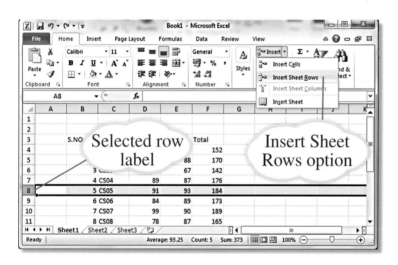

*Inserting a row in MS Excel 2010*

 OR

Select the row by clicking on the **row label**. Right-click on the mouse and choose the **Insert** option from the shortcut menu. A new row is added above the selected row.

## How to insert columns

1.  Select the **column label** before which a new column is to be inserted.
2.  Click on the **Home** tab.
3.  In the **Cells** group, click on the **Insert** drop-down list.
4.  From the drop-down list, select the **Insert Sheet Columns** option.
5.  A new column will be inserted before the selected column.

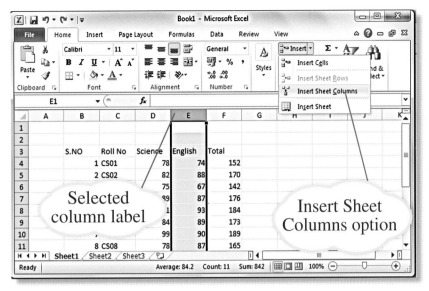

*Inserting a column in MS Excel 2010*

**OR**

Select the column by clicking on the **column label**. Right-click on the mouse, and choose the **Insert** option from the shortcut menu. A new column is added before the selected column.

---

**FACT FILE**

The total number of rows and columns in a worksheet cannot exceed the maximum limit. Data is shifted to the next row or column. If all the rows and the columns contain data and more data is added, then the data in the last row or column is deleted.

---

## Inserting Worksheets

You can shuffle between different worksheets using the **Sheet tabs**. These are found just above the Status Bar.

Sometimes, the default number of three sheets available are not enough for your work. To add more sheets, follow these steps.

1. Click on the **Home** tab.
2. In the **Cells** group, click on the **Insert** drop-down list.
3. From the drop-down list, select **Insert Sheet** option.
4. A new sheet will be inserted before the selected worksheet.

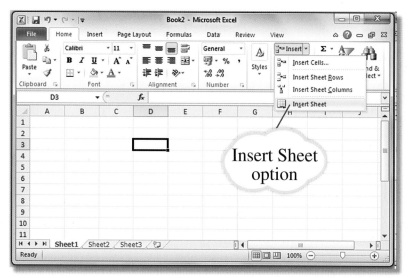

*Inserting a worksheet in MS Excel 2010*

**OR**

Click on the **Insert Worksheet** tab above the **Status Bar**. A new sheet named **Sheet4** will be inserted after the existing worksheets.

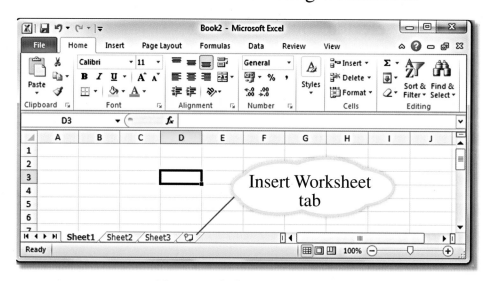

*New worksheets inserted*

**TRY THIS**

Right-click on a **Sheet** tab and select **Insert** from the shortcut menu. Select **Worksheet** in the **General** tab of the **Insert** dialog box. Click on **OK**.

**QUICK KEY**

| To insert a new worksheet in a workbook | **Shift + F11** |

# Inserting Cells

Adding a single cell or a collection of cells is allowed in a worksheet. When inserting new cells, the existing cells either shift to the right or down depending on the option selected. Follow these steps to insert cells in a worksheet.

1. Click on the **Insert** drop-down list in the **Cells** group of the **Home** tab.

2. Select the **Insert Cells** option from the drop-down list.

3. The **Insert** dialog box appears.

   The dialog box gives the following options.

   a. **Shift cells right**: Shifts the content of the selected cells to the right to make space for the new data.

   b. **Shift cells down**: Shifts the content of the selected cells down to make space for the new data.

   c. **Entire row**: Inserts a blank row by shifting the contents of the entire row down.

   d. **Entire column**: Inserts a blank column by shifting the contents of the entire column to the right.

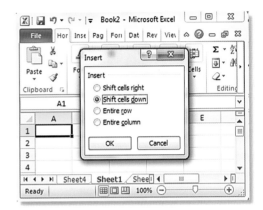

*Insert dialog box*

# Resizing Row Height and Column Width

Sometimes you need to alter the default height of a row and the width of a column. There are two ways to do this.

1. Resize the selected row by dragging the lower line of the row label up or down.

2. A selected column can be resized in a similar manner by dragging the line on the right of the column label inwards or outwards.

1. Click on the **row/column label**.

2. Go to **Home** tab ⟹ **Cells** group ⟹ **Format** drop-down list ⟹ **Row Height…/Column Width** option.

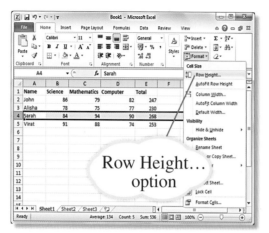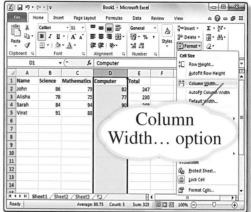

*Format row height and column width*

3. The **Row Height/Column Width** dialog box appears. Enter a numerical value for the height of the row/width of the column. Click on **OK**.

Type in the chosen row height

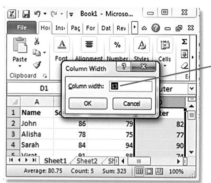

Type in the chosen column width

*Row Height and Column Width dialog boxes*

## Deleting Worksheets, Rows, Columns and Cells

### Deleting worksheets

1. Open the worksheet that needs to be deleted.
2. Click on the **Home** tab.
3. In the **Cells** group, click on the **Delete** drop-down list.

82

4.  Select the **Delete Sheet** option from the drop-down list.

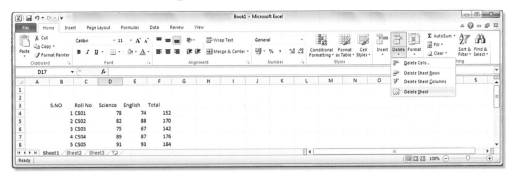

*Selecting Delete Sheet option*

5.  If the worksheet contains data, then the **Microsoft Office Excel** dialog box appears, asking for permission to delete both the worksheet and the data contained in it.

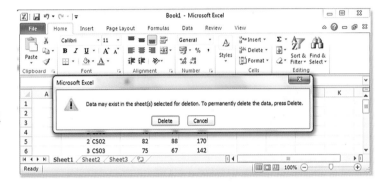

6.  Click **Delete** to confirm deletion.

*Microsoft Office Excel dialog box*

Right-click on the respective **Sheet tab**. Click the **Delete** option from the shortcut menu.

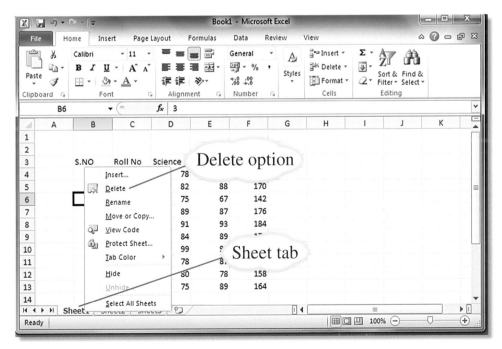

*Deleting a worksheet using the shortcut menu*

## Deleting rows

1. Select the row by clicking on the respective row label.
2. Click on the **Home** tab ⟹ **Cells** group ⟹ **Delete** drop-down list ⟹ **Delete Sheet Rows** option.

Right click on the row label. Select the **Delete** option from the shortcut menu.

## Deleting columns

1. Select the column by clicking on the respective column label.
2. Click on the **Home** tab ⟹ **Cells** group ⟹ **Delete** drop-down list ⟹ **Delete Sheet Columns** option.

Right-click on the column label. Select the **Delete** option from the shortcut menu.

## Deleting cells

1. Select the cell(s) you wish to delete.
2. Click on the **Home** tab ⟹ **Cells** group ⟹ **Delete** drop-down list ⟹ **Delete Cells** option.

Right-click on the selected cell(s). Select the **Delete** option from the shortcut menu.

3. In both the cases, the **Delete** dialog box appears. The dialog box gives the following options:

- **Shift cells left**: Overwrites the content by shifting the data from the cell on the right to the selected cell.
- **Shift cells up**: Overwrites the content by shifting the data from the cell below to the selected cell.
- **Entire row**: Overwrites the content by shifting the data from the row below. It appears that the entire row is deleted.

**TRY THIS**

To delete the contents of a cell, row or column, select the required portion and right-click to open the shortcut menu and click on the **Clear Contents** option to clear its content.

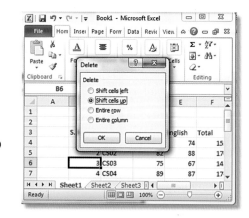

*Delete dialog box*

84

- **Entire column**: Overwrites the content by shifting the data from the column on the right. It appears that the entire column is deleted.
4.  Select the appropriate option. Click on the **OK** button.

## Alignment of Data in a Cell

This is the positioning of data within a cell. By fault, text is left aligned and numbers are right aligned. Broadly speaking, there are two types of alignments available. These are discussed here.

### Horizontal alignment

There are three types of horizontal alignment. These are Left, Center and Right.

### Vertical alignment

There are three types of vertical alignments. These are Top, Middle and Bottom.

You can change the alignment of data in a cell. Follow these steps.
1.  Select the cells.

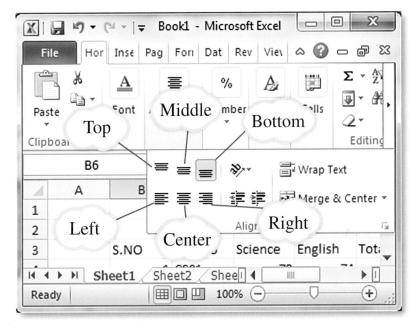

*Horizontal alignment and Vertical alignment*

2.  Click on the chosen alignment button in the **Alignment** group of the **Home** tab.

Complete the following activity.

1. Create a list of grades achieved by you in two internal assessments in all subjects.
2. Insert a column to contain the grades for the assessments in each subject.
3. Insert a row to add in the details of grades earned in Art.
4. Align the data in cells appropriately.
5. Format the data wherever possible.
6. Save the file as 'Myscore.xlsx'.

## Auto Fill Options

The Auto Fill feature allows you to quickly fill the cells with repetitive or sequential data such as chronological dates or numbers or repeated text. This feature is implemented by using the **Fill Handle** of the selected cell.

The cursor changes to 'plus' sign (+) when placed on the Fill Handle.

Follow these steps to quickly fill the cells with Auto Fill.

1. Select the cell with the chosen data and put the cursor on the small black square in the lower-right corner. A plus sign appears.

2. Drag it down to as many cells as you want to fill.

3. Release the mouse button. The **Auto Fill Options** box appears on the right of the plus sign.

4. Bring the cursor on the box and click on the drop-down arrow.

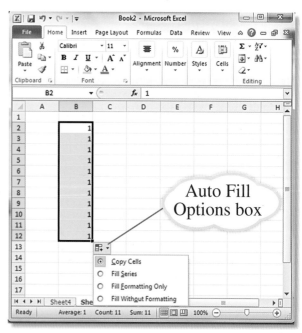

*Using Auto Fill*

5. Choose the appropriate action from the drop-down list. For example, click the **Fill Series** option to complete the series or the **Copy Cells** option to copy the contents of the selected cell.

> ### TRY THIS
>
> Auto Fill a column with cells containing the:
> 1. same number or date, with identical data in two adjacent cells (vertically or horizontally)
> 2. numbers in a series, with two values (vertically or horizontally)
>
> Select both the cells, click the left mouse button and drag to the desired cell. Release the mouse button.

The Auto Fill feature is not limited to numbers. It can also be used for text and a mix of text and numbers. For example, to make a repeating list of the days of the week:

1. Type 'Monday' in a cell.

2. Highlight the cell and drag across with the mouse.

3. Select the desired action from the **Auto Fill Options** drop-down list.

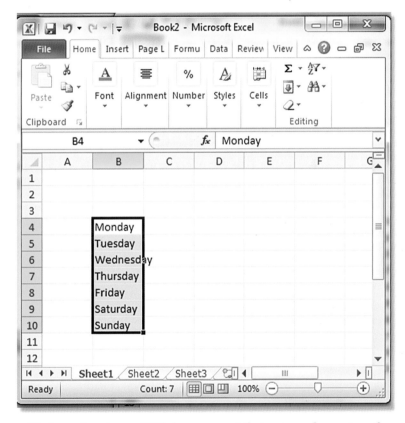

*Using the Auto Fill feature with text and a mix of text and numbers*

## Editing Data

### Selecting data

Before a cell can be modified or formatted, it must first be selected (highlighted).

Refer to the table given below for selecting groups of cells.

| Cells to select | Mouse action |
| --- | --- |
| One cell | Click once on a cell |
| Entire row | Click on the row label |
| Entire column | Click on the column label |
| Entire worksheet | Click on the entire sheet button (upper-left corner of the labels) |
| Range of cells | Drag mouse over the cells |

## Cutting cells

To cut cells, select the chosen cells and then click on the **Cut** option in the **Clipboard** group of the **Home** tab.

## Copying cells

To copy the cell contents, first select the cell and then click on the **Copy** option in the **Clipboard** group of the **Home** tab.

## Pasting cells

Select the cell into which you want to paste the content and then click on the **Paste** option in the **Paste** drop-down list in the **Clipboard** group of the **Home** tab.

ACTIVITY

Complete the following activity.
1. Open the file 'Myscore.xlsx' from the previous activity.
2. Insert a new column and give it the heading 'Project Grades'.
3. Copy and paste the grades from earlier columns to the new one.

# Saving an MS Excel 2010 File

After completing the work, you can save the changes in two ways.

1. Click on the **Save** button on the **Quick Access Toolbar**.

2. Choose a directory folder to save the file in.

3. Specify a file name, and then press **Save**.

1. Click on **File** tab drop-down list ⟹ **Save/Save As** option.

2. The **Save As** dialog box appears. Select the destination folder and specify the file name.

3. Click on the **Save** button.

*Save As dialog box*

It is recommended that you save your files every ten minutes.

When you save changes for the first time, you use **File** tab ⟹ **Save As** option.

After this, changes made in the same file are saved using the **Save** option in the **File** tab drop-down list.

# Opening an Already Saved MS Excel 2010 File

1. Click on the **File** tab.

2. Select **Open** from the drop-down list.

3. The **Open** dialog box appears. Click the source folder and select the chosen file in that folder.

4. Click on the **Open** button.

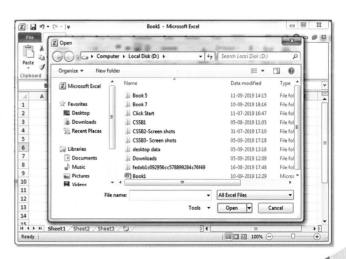

*Open dialog box*

## Opening a Blank Workbook in MS Excel 2010

1. Click on the **File** tab.

2. Select **New** option from the drop-down list.

3. The **New Workbook** dialog box appears. Select the **Blank Workbook** option from the **Available Templates**.

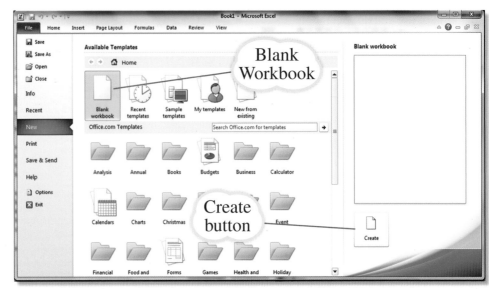

*Opening a new workbook*

4. Click on the **Create** button.

## Printing an MS Excel 2010 File

Follow these steps to print an MS Excel 2010 file:

1. Click on the **File** tab.

2. Select **Print** from the drop-down list.

3. The **Print** screen appears. Select the following options:

*Print dialog box*

   a. **Print range**    **All**

   b. **Print what**    **Selection** if any area is selected in the worksheet.

                       **Active sheet(s)** if current sheet is required to be printed.

                       **Entire workbook** if the whole workbook is required to be printed.

   c. **Copies**    **Number of copies** is 1 by default.

   d. **Preview**    To see the print preview before printing.

4. Click on **OK**.

It is recommended to see a print preview before printing to avoid any waste of paper.

## Exiting MS Excel 2010

1. Click on the **File** tab.
2. Select **Close** option from the drop-down list to close the current Excel workbook.

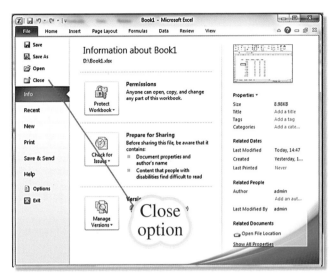

*Closing an MS Excel 2010 workbook*

 **OR**

Select the **Exit** option to exit the MS Excel 2010 application.

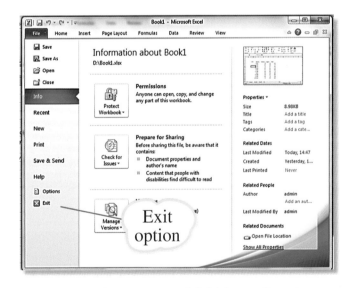

*Exiting the MS Excel 2010 application*

## ACTIVITY

Complete the following activity.

1. Save the worksheet created in the previous activity and name it 'Cars.xlsx'.
2. Close the file.　　3. Take a printout.　　4. Exit from Excel.

| | | | |
|---|---|---|---|
| One cell to the right | → | To the top edge of the current cell | Ctrl + ↑ |
| One cell to the left | ← | To the bottom edge of the current cell | Ctrl + ↓ |
| One cell down | ↓ | To the first cell in the row | Home |
| One cell up | ↑ | To the first cell in the worksheet | Ctrl + Home |
| To the right-hand edge of the current cell | Ctrl + → | To select the entire worksheet | Ctrl + A |
| To the left-hand edge of the current cell | Ctrl + ← | | |

## GLOSSARY

**Auto Fill**   A feature that fills the cells with repetitive or sequential data such as chronological dates or numbers or repeated text.

**Data**   A collection of values in the form of rows and columns.

**Fill Handle**   Allows the Auto Fill feature to be implemented to the selected cell.

**YOU ARE HERE**

**6**

1. MS Excel is the most popular spreadsheet package used to store data in the form of rows and columns.

2. A worksheet is a collection of cells in the form of rows and columns.

3. Each Excel file is known as a workbook that can hold many worksheets.

4. Columns are arranged vertically. These are headed with letters from A to Z and then AA to AZ and so on.

5. Rows are arranged horizontally. These are numbered from 1 to 1,048,576.

6. A cell is the intersection of a row and column.

7. A cell reference is the column letter and row number that identify a single cell.

8. The cell range is a selection of continuous cells.

9. The selected cell is called the Active Cell.

10. The Name Box displays the cell reference of the active cell.

11. The mouse pointer changes to a plus sign '✚' when it is on the worksheet.

12. The Formula Bar is found above the columns of the worksheet. It displays the formula or the data of an active cell.

13. Cells can contain text, numbers, or mathematical formulae. By default, text entries are aligned left and numbers are right aligned. In MS Excel, formulae begin with an 'equals to' (=) sign.

14. A cell, row, column or a worksheet can be inserted by using the Insert drop-down list in the Cells group of the Home tab.

15. A cell, row, column or a worksheet can be deleted by using the Delete drop-down list in the Cells group of the Home tab.

16. A cell, row or column can be resized by using the Format drop-down list in the Cells group of the Home tab.

17. The data in a cell can be aligned both vertically and horizontally.

18. The Auto Fill feature allows you to quickly fill the cells with repetitive or sequential data such as chronological dates or numbers or repeated text.

## EXERCISE

**A. Fill in the blanks.**

1. The Formula Bar displays the formula of an ..................... cell.

2. Columns in MS Excel are labelled as ..................... .

3. The mouse pointer changes to a ..................... sign on the worksheet.

4. The ..................... feature helps us to generate a data series.

5. A cell can be resized using the..................... option.

**B.   Give one word for each of the following.**

1.   Intersection of a row and a column     ...................................
2.   Extension of an Excel worksheet     ...................................
3.   A collection of continuous cells     ...................................
4.   First cell address of a worksheet     ...................................
5.   Bar that displays the formula     ...................................

**C.   True or false?**

1.   You cannot resize the column width.

2.   The Delete dialog box shows three options.

3.   Left, Right and Center are the three types of vertical alignments in MS Excel 2010.

4.   The Auto Fill feature can be used with numbers only.

5.   Editing of cells can be done using the Cut, Copy and Paste commands.

**D.   Name the following parts of the MS Excel 2010 Window.**

1.   ...................................
2.   ...................................
3.   ...................................
4.   ...................................
5.   ...................................
6.   ...................................
7.   ...................................
8.   ...................................
9.   ...................................

## E. Answer the following questions.

1. What is the default alignment of data in a worksheet?
2. What is the difference between a workbook and a worksheet?
3. Explain the Auto Fill feature in MS Excel 2010.
4. What are the different options available in the Insert dialog box?
5. How do you resize a cell in MS Excel 2010?

## LAB WORK

A. Create your class timetable in MS Excel 2010. Save it and take a printout.

B. Create an MS Excel 2010 spreadsheet of a list of purchases for a picnic.

1. The list should have the following headings: item name, price per item, quantity required and amount per item.

2. Calculate the total amount of pocket money spent for your picnic items.

C. Make a list of the cars you like in the given format:

| Car name | Company name | Cost | Color |
|---|---|---|---|
|  |  |  |  |
|  |  |  |  |

1. Add another column before the car name headed 'Serial no.'.

2. Use the Auto Fill feature to generate the serial numbers.

## PROJECT WORK

Create a list of the students in your class. Ask your subject teachers about all the information they maintain in their register, such as marks, remarks, parental information, parent-teacher's meeting, etc.

Insert that list in MS Excel and use all the formatting you have learnt so far.

- This is what the default window of MS Excel 2016 looks like. You can open an existing file, a blank file or select templates.

- If you select the Blank Workbook, the Ribbon design of MS Excel 2016 looks as shown below. By default, only Sheet1 is available in a book. But additional sheets can be inserted as required.

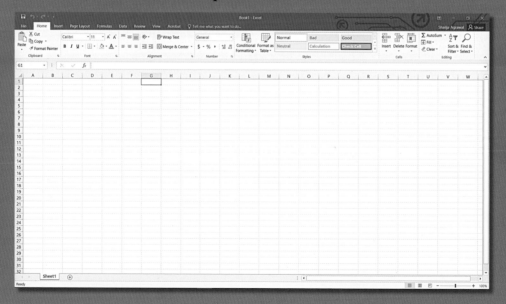

# The Internet

## Introduction

'Internet' stands for **interconnected network**. It is a vast network of computers which is made up of thousands of networks worldwide. The internet connects computers together, which enables the sharing of data communication services such as emails, chatting and file transfer. With increasing demand for ease of communication, the internet has become the most common medium of communication for millions of users. The internet was initially used by military and academic institutions but now it is a utility for everyone.

*Data communication services offered by the internet*

## History of the internet

The internet was initially known as ARPANET. It was implemented by the Department of Defence (DoD) of the United States of America. Later, it connected different universities of the USA. The main reason behind connecting universities and defence was to share information on research and development in scientific and military fields. It was a big success. Subsequently, it was made available commercially to everyone, with the new name 'internet'.

Network capable email was developed for the ARPANET shortly after its creation. It has now evolved into a powerful email technology, which is the most widely used application on the internet today.

## Who Governs the Internet?

The Internet is an interconnection of a number of computers with different types of networks across the globe. No one actually owns it. But there are three volunteer groups that were formed to help, coordinate and guide the technical parts of the Internet. These are:

Internet Activities Board (IAB)    Internet Engineering Task Force (IETF)

Internet Research Task Force (IRTF)

## Services Provided by the Internet
### Email

Email is an online correspondence system. It is a commonly used abbreviation for electronic mail. It allows computer users to exchange messages both locally and globally. The users have a mailbox address. For example, abc@cambridge.org. Messages sent through email can arrive within a few seconds, unlike traditional mail that can take days or weeks to deliver. Email provides the option to send electronic files to a person's email address or even to yourself for retrieval at a different location. In this way, information sharing and retrieval is available anywhere with access to the internet. Email is also excellent for keeping in touch with family and friends.

The advantages of email over telephone, fax and postal services are as follows:

1. It is fast.
2. There is no charge per use.

*Drafting an email*

## Information

The internet is a virtual treasure trove of information. There is a huge amount of information available on the internet about every subject. It may range from government laws and services, trade fairs and conferences, market information and new ideas for technical support.

The 'search engines' on the internet can help you to find data on any subject that you need. Google, Yahoo and Bing are examples of such search engines.

## Services

Many services are now provided on the internet such as online banking, job search and applications, along with online reservations for movies, railways and airlines. Often these services are either not available offline or cost more.

When you are connected to the internet, you are online, otherwise you are in an offline mode.

## Buy or sell products

You can buy and sell products all over the world through the internet. This is called **online shopping**. There are many online stores and sites that can be browsed to see the products that can be bought. You don't need to leave your house, and can do your shopping from the convenience of your home.

> **FACT FILE**
>
> Any kind of business can operate through the internet. New products can be launched, promoted and advertised. Customers can buy and sell products through the internet. This is also known as **e-business**. Buying and selling of products through the internet is called **e-commerce**.

## Communities

Online communities are a popular forum on the internet to meet up with people who have similar interests and discuss common issues. There are various social networking sites where people can connect with their family and friends in one place. Communities of all types have sprung up on the internet.

## Online chat

People all over the world can communicate with each other online on websites that use internet chat software. This is known as **e-chat** and it is interactive. As you type the message on the screen and send, you immediately receive a reply from the other user who is logged in.

*e-chat*

There are many 'chat rooms' on the web where you can interact with multiple users at the same time. These are a popular way to meet new people, make new friends, as well as to stay in touch with old friends. Chatrooms may be used to spread awareness and exchange ideas about a specific cause. For example, there are science forums within a chat room where you can exchange your ideas on global warming, conservation of wildlife, etc.

## Downloading data

Getting data from the host computer (server) to the client computer (user's computer) is known as **downloading**. You can download innumerable games, music, videos, movies, and a host of other informative and entertainment software from the internet, most of which are free.

A host computer (server) is the one where all the data or information related to the internet is stored. The client computer (user's computer) is the one that you use.

## Uploading data

Copying the data from the client computer (user's computer) to the host computer (server) is known as **uploading**. This process is generally used when you want to send photographs, articles or files to your friends, family, etc.

## Online backup

You can store all your files online using the online backup system provided by **Online Backup Providers** like Dropbox and Google Drive. You can access these files from anywhere and at any time.

**ACTIVITY**

Explore the wonderful animal kingdom with the help of the internet. Download interesting information and pictures for the animals shown here.

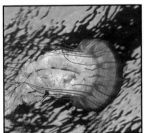   

## Basic Internet Terms

Let us learn about some important terms related to the internet.

**FACT FILE**

Moving from one website to another is known as **net surfing**.

### Internet Service Providers (ISP)

An Internet Service Provider (ISP) is a company that offers its customers access to the internet. An ISP connects to its customers using a data transmission technology appropriate for delivering internet services such as dial up, wireless, modem or dedicated high-speed interconnections. For example, MTNL, Airtel and Vodafone.

## Modem

As you learnt in the first chapter, a modem is a device that allows communication with other computers. The speed of a

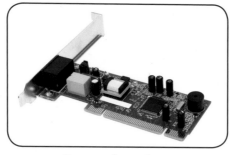

*Internal modem*

*External modem*

modem is measured in bps (bits per second). There are two types of modem.

1. **Internal Modem**: fitted inside a computer.
2. **External Modem**: placed outside the computer.

## Protocols

Protocols are the set of rules that has to be followed for communicating data in the networking environment. An example of a protocol used for computers to communicate through the Internet is TCP/IP.

## World Wide Web (WWW)

The World Wide Web (WWW) is a system or collection of interlinked pages that can be accessed through the internet for information by anyone across the globe. These interlinked pages are called **web pages** and contain text, audio, graphics, links to other pages, etc. The World Wide Web has enabled the spread of information over the internet through an easy-to-use and flexible format. It has played an important role in popularising the use of the internet.

**FACT FILE**

The WWW was developed by Sir Tim Berners-Lee in 1989.

## Search engines

A web search engine is a computer program used to search for information on the World Wide Web (WWW) or the internet by looking for keywords or a set of words which the user has typed in.

The search results are usually presented in a list, and are commonly called **hits**. The information may consist of web pages, images, data and other types of files.

*Google search engine*

A search engine like Google not only gives users the opportunity to search for content on different topics, but also has many more interesting features like maps, blogs, calendar etc.

The toolbar on the top of the Google screen has the following options.

**Images**: To find pictures related to the keywords written in the search box.

**Maps**: To find routes, view landmarks and buildings, find specific locations, etc.

**Play**: To buy android apps, e-books, movies and devices.

**YouTube**: To search for videos and music.

**News**: To get the latest news from across the world.

**Gmail**: To access an email account.

**Drive**: To synchronise different computers and mobile devices, so that the data is available to the user anywhere and at all times.

**Calendar**: A virtual planner that allows the user to schedule and plan events, meetings, etc. which can be shared at the workplace, or with friends and family. It sends alerts via messages and emails to a computer or phone.

**More**: This button offers a variety of options to choose from. A user can read online e-books, translate content from one language to another and learn its pronunciation, shop online, create their own blog, etc.

## Web browser

A web browser is a Graphical User Interface (GUI), like Internet Explorer, Mozilla Firefox, Google Chrome and Opera. It can also be text-based, like Lynx, that allows the user to open websites. In other words, a web browser, or simply 'browser' is an application used to access and view websites.

## Home page

The home page is the first page or main page of the hypertext document. This page is the address of a file that automatically loads when a web browser starts or when the browser's 'Home' button is pressed.

## URL

URL stands for **Uniform Resource Locator**, and is also referred to as a **web address**. The URL specifies the internet address of a file stored on a host computer or server connected to the internet. Web browsers use the URL to retrieve the file from the server. This file is downloaded to the user's (client) computer and displayed on the monitor connected to the machine. Every file on the internet, no matter what its protocol is, has a unique URL.

*URL*

**FACT FILE**

URLs are translated into numeric addresses using the **Domain Name System** (DNS). The numeric address, called the IP (Internet Protocol) address, is actually the 'real' URL. Since numeric strings are difficult to use, alphanumeric addresses are employed by end users.

## Web page

A web page is a hypertext document which has a collection of audio, text, images and video inserted in it. It can be accessed through a web browser and displayed on a computer screen.

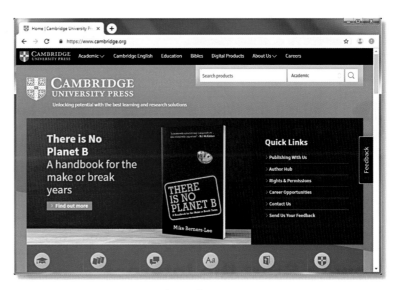

*A webpage*

## Website

A website is a collection of related web pages, images, videos or even sounds that have a common web address. Here, you get information on a set of web pages about a particular subject which has been published by the same person or organisation. It often contains pictures, videos and sound.

A website is hosted on at least one web server, accessible via the internet.

For example, google.com, discovery.com and cambridge.org.

## Hyperlinks

You can view web pages that may contain text, images, videos, etc. with the help of a web browser. You can navigate between them using special links called **hyperlinks**. For example, you may click on the Contact us hyperlink to visit the Contact us page on the Cambridge University Press website, www.cambridge.org.

## HyperText Transfer Protocol (HTTP)

Hypertext Transfer Protocol (HTTP) is a set of rules that gives users access to transfer hyperlinked or hypertext documents over the internet. It gives users access to email services and gives space on the internet to show documents. Some ISPs are free and give you as many email addresses as you want, but for others you need to subscribe.

A. Find out the type of modem you use at home.

B. Domain names may be country specific also. For example, Japanese websites have a secondary extension of 'jp'. Search for some good educational websites in the USA, Canada and Australia. You might want to first search the Internet for country domain name extensions.

## How to Start the Internet

In order to view a website, you must first open a web browser where you enter the URL of the website.

To view the website, you need to follow the steps given below.

1. Click on **Start** ⟹ **All Programs** ⟹ **Internet Explorer**.

2. In the **Address Bar**, enter the website address or the URL.

3. For example, the website www.cambridge.org is shown here.

*The website www.cambridge.org*

### FACT FILE

The extension of the web address or domain name gives you the information about the type of site. For example, .com stands for commercial, .edu for educational, and .org for a non-profit organisation.

# Internet Explorer

Internet Explorer is a series of graphical web browsers developed by Microsoft. It was included as part of the Microsoft Windows line of operating systems in 1995. It has been one of the most widely used web browsers since then.

Internet Explorer opens just like any other software window. The different components of the default window of Internet Explorer are:

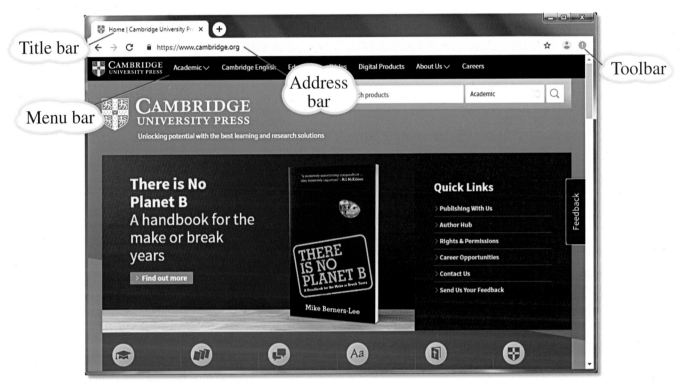

*Components of a window opened using Internet Explorer*

## Backward tool

When you have browsed multiple pages and you wish to move to the previous page, the Backward tool is used.

## Forward tool

After viewing previous web pages, to move to the next page click on the Forward tool.

**FACT FILE**

The browser will not be able to access any website if the computer is not connected to an ISP (Internet Service Provider).

### Stop tool ✕

The Stop tool is used to stop the browsing of any website.

### Refresh tool 🔃

When the web page information needs to be updated on the screen, the Refresh tool can be used. This tool refreshes the page by sending the information again.

### Favorites tool ☆ Favorites

This tool allows the user to organise and keep records of important or frequently visited websites and web pages.

### Home tool 🏠

This brings the user back to the home page.

### Tools button Tools ▾

Allows the user to access features like Print, History, Settings, etc.

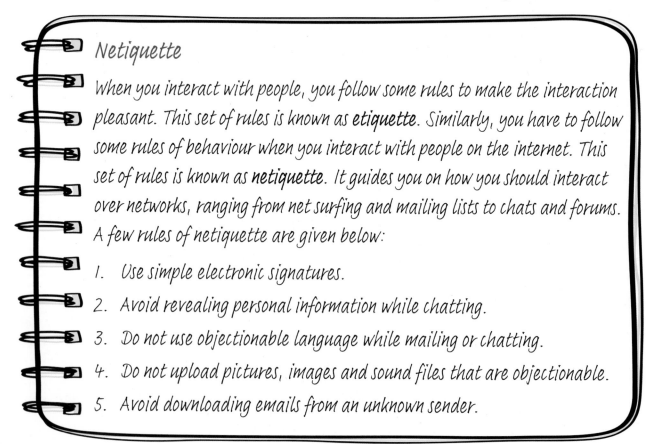

*Netiquette*

*When you interact with people, you follow some rules to make the interaction pleasant. This set of rules is known as **etiquette**. Similarly, you have to follow some rules of behaviour when you interact with people on the internet. This set of rules is known as **netiquette**. It guides you on how you should interact over networks, ranging from net surfing and mailing lists to chats and forums. A few rules of netiquette are given below:*

1. *Use simple electronic signatures.*
2. *Avoid revealing personal information while chatting.*
3. *Do not use objectionable language while mailing or chatting.*
4. *Do not upload pictures, images and sound files that are objectionable.*
5. *Avoid downloading emails from an unknown sender.*

# Viruses

A **computer virus** is a program or a piece of code that is loaded onto your computer without your knowledge. It makes the computer run against your instructions. Viruses can also replicate themselves and multiply. All computer viruses are man-made. A simple virus that can replicate itself over and over again is relatively easy to produce. Even a simple virus is dangerous because it will quickly use all the computer's available memory and bring the system to a halt. An even more dangerous type of virus is one capable of transmitting itself across networks and bypassing security systems.

An **internet virus** is a program that is sent to different people through the internet in the form of emails or links. These are sent to harm computer systems. You may receive an email with the subject 'Very Important',

and the moment you open it, the system will crash. These computer viruses behave the same way as biological viruses by contaminating any computer systems they come in contact with. These self-executing programs are generally very small and damage the way your computer works.

Many **anti-virus** programs are available, such as Norton AntiVirus, Kasper Sky and Quick Heal. These are used to protect the main memory of a computer against infection by a virus.

Anti-virus programs periodically check your computer system for the most common types of viruses. Having a good anti-virus program and current updates is one of the best ways to protect your computer system against virus attacks.

## Cyber Security

Organisations across the globe rely on information technology for creating and sharing information. An unauthorised person can interfere with data security to access data and might become a threat to the integrity and confidentiality of a system. **Cyber security** is used to protect computers and data connected through the network/internet from an unauthorised user. It helps to prevent data from being stolen or damaged.

The techniques used in cyber security protect:

- hardware like laptops, desktop PCs and servers.
- software like applications and programs.
- data stored on the network.

## ACTIVITY

Complete the following activity.

1. Type http://www.google.com in the Address bar.

2. Now type 'List of Viruses and Anti-viruses on the Internet' in the search box. Click on the **Google Search** button.

3. You will see a list of websites. Make a list of five virus and anti-virus programs with a brief description of each of them.

4. Do you know any other website which works as a search engine? Find at least three of them.

## QUICK KEY

| | |
|---|---|
| To move to the next tab in any browser with multiple tabs opened | **Ctrl + Tab** |
| To open a homepage | **Alt + Home** |

# GLOSSARY

**Anti-virus**  A program used to protect the main memory of a computer against infection by a virus.

**Downloading**  The process of getting data from the server to the user's computer.

**Email**  An online correspondence system.

**Home page**  The address of a file that automatically loads when a web browser starts.

**Internet Explorer**  A series of graphical web browsers developed by Microsoft.

**Internet Service Provider**  A company responsible for offering internet services.

**Internet Virus**  A program that is sent to different people through the Internet in the form of emails or links.

**Netiquette**  A set of practices to be followed to make the experience of using the Internet safe and pleasant for everyone.

**Offline**  When you are not connected to the internet.

**Online**  When you are connected to the internet.

**Protocols**  A set of rules followed for communicating data in a networking environment.

**Uniform Resource Locator (URL)**  The internet address of a file stored on a host computer connected to the internet.

**Uploading**  The process of copying data from the user's computer to the server.

**Virus**  A program or piece of code that makes the computer run against your instructions.

**Web page**  A page of information on the internet about a particular topic that forms part of a website.

**Website**  A collection of related web pages, images, videos, etc. that have a common web address.

**Web search engine**  A computer program to search for information on the World Wide Web.

**World Wide Web**  A system of interconnected documents accessed via the internet.

1. The internet is a system of connecting computers together, enabling them to share information.

2. The internet is a virtual source of information.

3. Many services are now provided on the internet such as online banking, job search and applications, hotel reservations, online shopping and communities.

4. There are many chat rooms on the web that can be accessed to meet new people, make new friends, and to stay in touch with old friends.

5. You can download games, music, videos, movies, and other entertainment software from the internet, many of which are free.

6. To view a website you must open a web browser where you enter the URL of the website.

7. Internet Explorer opens just like any other software window. It has the Title bar, Menu bar, Toolbar, Address bar and Status bar.

8. There are various tools present on Internet Explorer such as the Backward tool, Forward tool, Refresh tool and Home tool.

9. Anti-virus programs periodically check your computer system for known types of viruses.

**EXERCISE**

**A. True or false?**

1. Email is an online correspondence system.

2. Downloading is generally used when you want to send photographs, articles or files to your friends, family, etc.

3. The speed of a modem is measured in kilometres per second.

4. Search results are usually presented in a list, and are commonly called hits.

5. Internet Explorer is a series of graphical web browsers developed by Microsoft.

6. An Anti-virus is a program or a piece of code that is loaded onto your computer without your knowledge.

## B. Solve the crossword using the given clues.

**Across**

4. An example of an Online Backup Provider.

6. Getting the data from the host computer (server) to the client computer (user's computer) is known as …………

7. A ………… is a device that allows communication with other computers.

**Down**

1. A URL is also referred to as a ………… address.

2. The internet was initially known as ………… .

3. ………… are the set of rules that has to be followed for communicating data in the networking environment.

5. ………… is a vast network of computers which is made up of thousands of networks worldwide.

## C. Identify the tools and state their purpose.

| Icon | Name of the tool | Purpose of the tool |
|------|------------------|---------------------|
| 1. | | |
| 2. | | |
| 3. | | |
| 4. | | |
| 5. ☆ Favorites | | |

**D. Match the following.**

| | | | | |
|---|---|---|---|---|
| 1. | IAB | a. | Uniform Resource Locator |
| 2. | URL | b. | Internet Activities Board |
| 3. | ISP | c. | Hypertext Transfer Protocol |
| 4. | WWW | d. | Internet Service Provider |
| 5. | HTTP | e. | World Wide Web |

**E. Answer the following questions.**

1. Explain any two uses of the internet.
2. Name three governing groups of the internet.
3. State the difference between a computer virus and an internet virus.
4. List any three rules of netiquette.
5. Discuss the importance of Internet Explorer.

**LAB WORK**

A. Open the website cartoonnetwork.com and check the timings of your favourite cartoon program.

B. Open the website www.discovery.com and try to find out some latest facts.

C. Open the website www.cambridge.org and explore it.

D. Make a list of four web browsers other than Internet Explorer that can be used to surf or explore the internet. Gather some interesting facts about each and write the information in the following format:
  • Name of the browser:
  • Logo:
  • Designed and owned by (company or person's name):
  • Important features:

E. Email is an important feature of the internet. Find out the list of websites that provide you with the facility of creating and maintaining your email accounts. Write a few lines about each.

F. How do you access the Internet at your school and at home? Try to find out the name of the Internet Service Providers and the advantages and disadvantages of each. Make a presentation on this.

## PROJECT WORK

Why is cyber security important in the world of the internet?

Create a brochure/poster on the topic of Cyber Security. Insert a few pictures, and you may use the internet to find some information.

### WHO AM I?

I was born on 21 August 1973 in Moscow and moved to the United States in 1979.

With my business partner Larry Page, we started the Google search engine. The aim was to search the web efficiently and provide more relevant results than the search engines available at that time.

I am ...................................

# Learning Algorithms

## 8

## Introduction

Welcome to the world of programming! You have already learnt that a program is a set of instructions written to perform a specific task. When you are assigned to do a task you need to follow a series of steps in the right order. In this lesson, you will learn the language to write down the steps to perform any specific task.

## Algorithms

Algorithms can be defined as the process or set of rules to be followed in calculations or other problem-solving operations, especially by a computer. The first step in every programming language is to write an algorithm. Let us first understand the term 'algorithm'.

For example, your teacher has asked you to collect some dry leaves for a science project. To do this task, you need to follow the steps below:

Go to the nearest park/garden
↓
Collect the fallen leaves
↓
Take the leaves home
↓
Wrap the leaves in an old newspaper for a few days to dry
↓
Take the dried leaves to school

In doing any task, certain steps have to be followed. In computing, this is called an **algorithm**. *An algorithm is the step-by-step process for doing a task. It produces an ordered sequence of steps that provides a solution to a problem.*

An algorithm is an effective method of solving a problem using a sequence of instructions. Algorithms form a fundamental part of computing. Before you start understanding a computer language, you need to learn algorithms. You will realise that it is easier to understand the logic of a program if it is done through algorithms.

## Advantages of algorithms

1. **Easy to understand**: An algorithm is a step-by-step procedure for problem solving, which makes it easier to understand.
2. **Independent of programming language**: An algorithm is written in simple English statements to depict the logic of a problem and it is not based on any programming language.
3. **Easy to debug**: Every step in an algorithm has its own logical sequence which makes it easier to debug (to spot errors).

## Disadvantages of algorithms

1. **Time-consuming**: It is a time-consuming technique.
2. **Not suitable for all problems**: An algorithm is not suitable for solving certain problems, such as looping (see page 122) and branching.
3. **Difficult for bigger problems**: Algorithms are not preferred for solving bigger problems as they are very time-consuming.

## Tools of algorithms

The two commonly used tools to understand the program logic are:

Flowchart    Pseudocode

You may use both these methods as problem-solving techniques. Generally, a flowchart is used for simple problems and pseudocode is used for complex problems.

# Flowcharts

Flowcharts are a graphical representation of algorithms.

Flowcharts use shapes as symbols to represent an activity. The flow lines with arrows are used to depict the flow of data within a program. A flowchart emphasises individual steps and their interconnections within a program. The various symbols used in a flowchart are given in the table below.

| Name | Symbol | Description |
| --- | --- | --- |
| Terminator box | (Oval) | Represents the beginning or the end of a flowchart. |
| Input/Output box | (Parallelogram) | Represents the input and output operations in a flowchart. |
| Process box | (Rectangle) | Represents the process or an instruction to be carried out. For example, addition or calculation. |
| Decision box | (Diamond) | This symbol is used in branching when a decision is to be made. |
| Connector box | | This connects one part of the flowchart to another. |
| Flow lines | | These represent the flow of information from one point to another. |

## Guidelines

The following are some guidelines for flowcharting.

1. The listing of all requirements should be done in a logical order.
2. Ensure that the flowchart has a logical start and finish.
3. The flow of information in a flowchart should be from top to bottom or from left to right.

4. Only one flow line should come out from a process symbol.

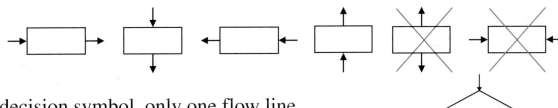

5. In a decision symbol, only one flow line should enter it, whereas there can be any number of outgoing flow lines.

6. The terminator symbol can have only one flow line.

7. Connectors reduce the number of flow lines. These should be used to make the flowchart simple. Avoid the intersection of flow lines.

8. The flowchart should be clear and easy to follow.

On the right is a flowchart for the science project at the start of the chapter.

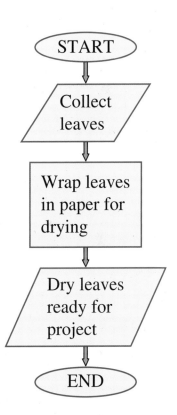

## Advantages of flowcharts

- The symbols are self-explanatory and easier to understand.
- Graphic symbols make the process of explaining an algorithm quite straightforward.
- With the help of a flowchart, problems can be analysed in a more effective way.

## Disadvantages of flowcharts

- Diagrammatic representation takes a lot of time.
- Difficult to handle complex programs.
- Standard rules need to be followed for making a flowchart.
- If changes are required, the flowchart may need to be completely redrawn.

## ACTIVITY

Draw a flowchart for the following tasks.

1. Buying a pair of jeans.

2. Calculating the area of a circle.

3. Calculating the perimeter of a rectangle.

## Pseudocode

Pseudocode means 'false code'. It is an informal language that helps programmers to develop algorithms. It is generally written in simple English statements to represent the logic of a program. Pseudocode helps a non-programmer to understand how a program works. There is no uniform pseudocode language. One person's pseudocode can differ from that of the other.

Let us take a situation where you want to write a pseudocode for calculating the area of a rectangle. The pseudocode to calculate the area of the rectangle is shown on the right.

```
Begin
    Input Length, Breadth
    Calculate Area = Length*Breadth
    Display Area
End
```

### Advantages of pseudocode

• Closer to programming code, so easier to understand.

• Can be used as a starting point or outline for writing real code.

• Pseudocode can be constructed quickly as compared to a flowchart.

### Disadvantages of pseudocode

• Since no standards are used, it is difficult to maintain consistency.

• It is difficult to understand and manipulate.

# Types of Programming Statements

The set of instructions written in an algorithm are basically of three types.

## Sequential

All the algorithms done up until now fall under the sequential category. The statements are executed (run) one after the other, in the sequence in which they are written. The statements written first are executed first.

## Conditional

When the flow of control of the program is based on a condition, you make use of conditional statements.

For example, to order at a restaurant:

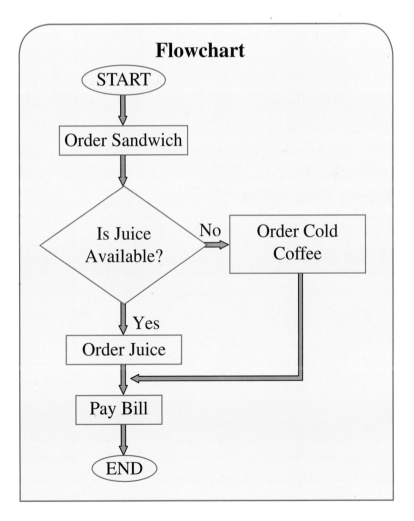

**Pseudocode**

Begin
    Order Sandwich
    Is Juice available
        Order Juice
    Else
        Order Cold Coffee
    End if
    Pay the bill
End

**Flowchart**

## Iterations or Loops

Sometimes there is a need to repeat a set of statements more than once based on a certain condition. This process of repetition is called a loop or an iteration.

For example, conditional display of "Hello":

**Pseudocode**

Begin

    Let I = 1

    Do While I <= 5

        Display "Hello"

        Change I = I + 1

    End loop

    Display "Program Over"

End

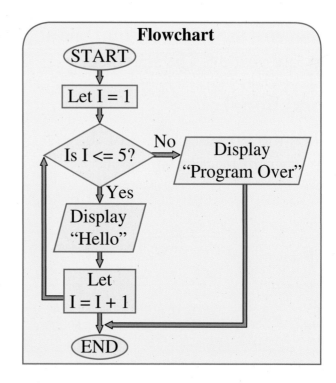

## Some examples

*Example 1*: To display the sum of two numbers.

**Pseudocode**

Begin

    Input A, B

    Calculate Sum = A + B

    Display Sum

End

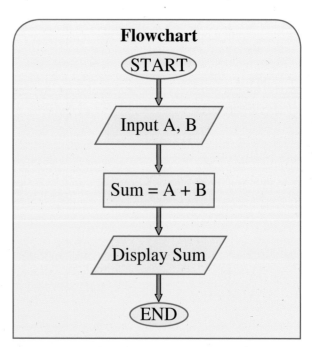

*Example 2*: To display the average of three numbers.

**Pseudocode**

Begin

    Input A, B, C

    Calculate Average = (A + B + C)/3

    Display Average

End

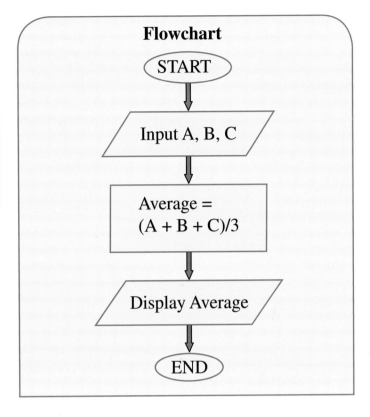

*Example 3*: To find the smaller of two given numbers.

**Pseudocode**

Begin

    Input A, B

    If A is smaller than B

        Display A

    Otherwise

        Display B

    End if

End

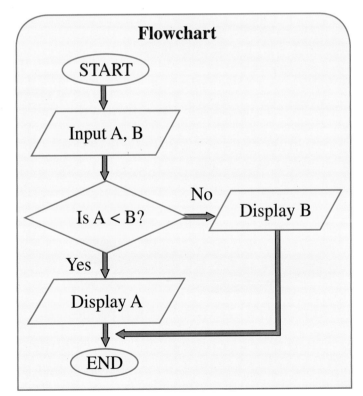

*Example 4*: To display even numbers from 1 to 10.

**Pseudocode**

Begin

    Let C = 2

    Do While C <= 10

        Display C

        Let C = C + 2

    End Loop

    Display "Program Over"

End

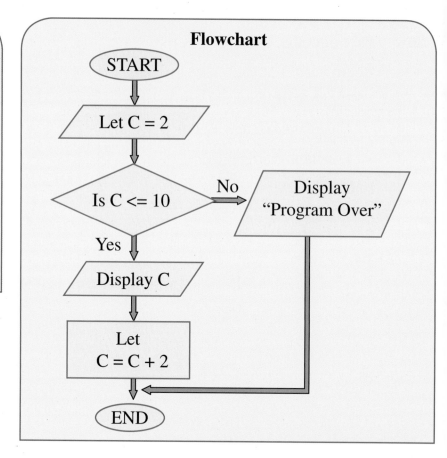

**Flowchart**

## ACTIVITY

Draw a flowchart for the following tasks:

1. Calculating the product of two numbers.

2. Calculating the percentage of any three subjects.

## GLOSSARY

**Algorithm**  A step-by-step process of doing a task.

**Flowchart**  A graphical representation of an algorithm.

**Loop**  The process of repetition based on certain conditions.

**Pseudocode**  'False' code. An informal language written in simple English statements to help programmers develop algorithms.

1. The tools of the algorithm are flowcharts and pseudocode.

2. Flowcharts use shapes as symbols to represent an activity.

3. Pseudocode is an informal language that helps programmers develop algorithms.

4. The set of instructions written in an algorithm are basically of three types.

   a. Sequential – The step-by-step procedure to write the instructions.

   b. Conditional – When the flow of control of the program is based on a condition.

   c. Iteration or a Loop – To repeat a set of statements more than once based on a certain condition.

## EXERCISE

### A. True or false?

1. The last step of every programming language is to write an algorithm.

2. Flowcharts are the graphical representation of an algorithm.

3. Flowcharts use numbers as symbols to represent an activity.

4. Pseudocode is a formal language that helps non-programmers develop algorithms.

5. When the flow of control of the program is based on a condition, we make use of a sequential algorithm.

## B. Fill in the blanks.

1. An ............... is a step-by-step process of doing a task.
2. .................... means false code.
3. ................. is the process of repetition based on certain conditions.
4. The tools of the algorithm are .................. and .................. .
5. .................... does not follow any standard for writing the instructions.

## C. Write the pseudocode to play snakes and ladders. The steps given below are not in order.

1. Landed on snake head?
2. Slide down the snake
3. Climb up ladder
4. Reached 100?
5. Move your coin
6. Throw the dice
7. At bottom of ladder?

## D. Spot and fix the errors in the following pseudocode.

1. Begin
        Let C = 3
        Do While C >=10
        Display C
        Let C = C + + 2
        End Loop
        Disp "End of Program"
    End

2. Begin
        Input Length, Breadth
        Calculate Area =
        Length*Breadth*Height
        Display Volume
    Exit

## E. Answer the following questions.

1. What is meant by an algorithm?
2. What is a flowchart? Make a symbol to represent a process and an input.
3. Give any two advantages and disadvantages of using a flowchart.
4. What is pseudocode? Give an example.
5. Discuss the types of programming statements.
6. Draw a flowchart and write the pseudocode to read English consonants until the user wishes to stop the input.

## LAB WORK

**A.** Write the pseudocode and make a flowchart for the following in MS Word 2010:

1. Input three numbers and find out the largest of the three.
2. Input a number and check whether it is even or odd.
3. Input marks and display whether failed or passed.
4. Display natural numbers from 1 to 10.
5. Display even numbers from 20 to 40.
6. Input a number and display the next five consecutive numbers.
7. Input a number and display the table of a number.

**B.** Look at the flowchart on the right. Write the pseudocode that best describes the process.

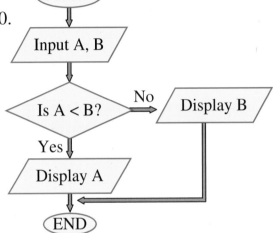

## PROJECT WORK

Create a chart explaining the symbols used in a flowchart.

---

## WHO AM I?

I was born in England in 1815. As a young girl, I took an interest in mathematics and, in particular, Babbage's work on the analytical engine.

I am considered to be the first computer programmer. I described how Babbage's analytical engine could be programmed.

I am ....................................

# Introduction to Scratch

**9**

## SNAP RECAP

1. What is a 'programming language'?
2. List some programming languages.

## LEARNING OBJECTIVES

*You will learn about:*

- how to start Scratch
- components of a Scratch window
- how to change, move or add sounds to Sprites
- saving a project
- opening a new project
- exiting Scratch

## Introduction

Scratch is a visual programming language. It is based on a drag and drop feature which makes it suitable to create games, animated stories and projects. The Scratch language provides in-built graphic characters which can perform actions according to the commands given. These characters are called **Sprites**. These Sprites are similar to the Turtle in Logo. This chapter uses Scratch 2.0. For Scratch 3.0 updates, go to the end of the chapter.

## Why Scratch?

Scratch is used as an introductory programming language because it makes the creation of animated stories and games an easy task. With the help of blocks, programming skills can be learnt easily.

### FACT FILE

Scratch was developed by the Lifelong Kindergarten Group at the MIT Media lab, led by Mitchel Resnick in 2003. However the first official website of Scratch was launched in 2006. It is a free software program.

The features of Scratch are listed below:

- It is available free of charge.
- It is easy to learn and understand.
- It is independent of an operating system.
- There is no need to write commands; predefined blocks are snapped together to create the script.

## How to start Scratch

To start Scratch, visit the Scratch website, scratch.mit.edu. You can then click 'Start creating' to open the Scratch window with the Editor screen. You can also download the Scratch App from the same website, so you can use Scratch offline.

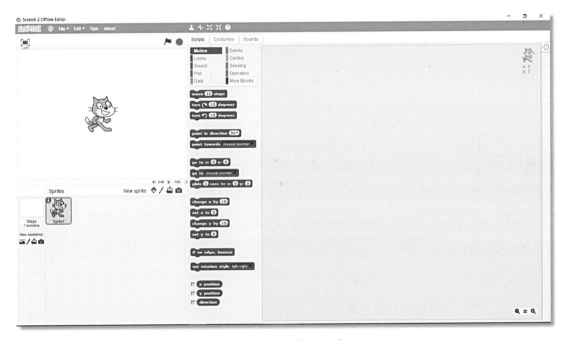

*The Scratch (2.0) window*

## Components of the Scratch Window

You will now learn about the various components of the Scratch window.

**Title Bar**: Found at the top of the window, this bar shows the title of the application being used.

**Menu Bar**: This displays the list of menus available for the application. They are the drop-down menus that can be accessed by the mouse or with the keyboard.

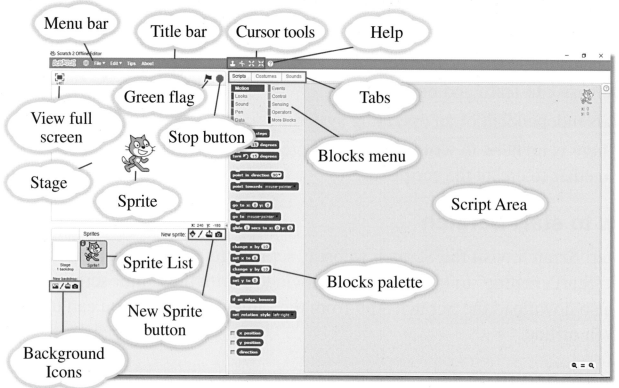

*Components of the Scratch window*

**Blocks Palette**: Contains the various predefined blocks that are used to perform specific tasks.

*x* and *y* coordinates: These coordinates indicate the position of a Sprite on the stage. The point at which the two axes meet is the centre of the stage. Origin is the centre of the stage where both *x* axis and *y* axis is 0.

**Tabs**: There are three tabs in Scratch – **Scripts**, **Costumes** and **Sounds**. All of them perform a specific task. An additional tab, **Backdrops**, appears only when we select the Stage icon to add any in-built background.

**Script Area**: The collection of step-wise instructions given to a Sprite is called a Script (Scratch 2.0) or Code (Scratch 3.0). The place where we pick and drop the blocks to create the Script is called a Script Area.

**The Stage**: This is the actual area to draw or perform actions. The Stage is the area where the Sprite moves. The position of the Sprite on the Stage is referred to using (*x*, *y*) coordinates. The coordinates can be seen at the bottom right corner of the Stage.

**Green Flag**: Used to start the execution of all scripts in the project.

**Stop Button**: Used to stop the execution of the block.

**Current Sprite Information**: Includes information about the selected Sprite and as well as tools for controlling the Sprite. The tools include:

- Circular Arrow: Sprite can be rotated fully.
- Linear Arrow: Allows the Sprite to face left or right.
- Disable Rotation: It disables the rotation of the Sprite so that it is fixed to 90 degrees.

**Sprite Direction**: It specifies the direction of the Sprite when a move instruction is given.

## Adding a New Sprite

After opening the Scratch window, by default the Cat Sprite appears on the stage. However we can create, import or use the available Sprites in our project. Select the **New sprite** option located at the bottom right corner of the Stage.

- **Choose sprite from library**: Contains many exciting in-built Sprite options.
- **Paint new sprite**: Selecting this button will open the **Paint editor window**, where you can draw a new Sprite.

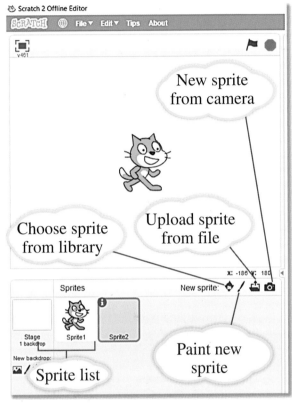

*Adding a new Sprite*

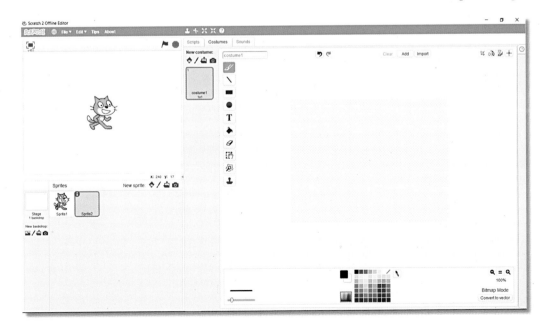

*Paint editor window*

131

- **Upload sprite from file** Clicking this button will open the **Select file(s) to upload by app:/Scratch.swf** dialog box that allows you to select a Sprite from the files stored on your computer.

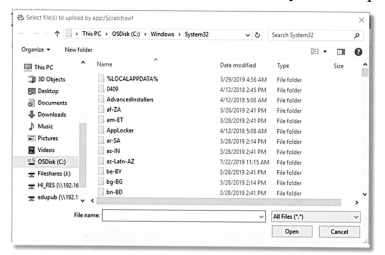

*Select File(s) to upload by app:/Scratch.swf dialog box*

**TRY THIS**

Create a Sprite with your name by taking a picture of yourself with a webcam.

- **New sprite from camera**: This option allows the user to use the web camera of the computer to take a picture and use it as a Sprite.

- **Sprite list**: Located below the Stage. The Sprite list displays the thumbnails of all the Sprites that are available for the project.

## Steps to Start a New Project

1. Select **File** tab ⟹ **New** option from the menu bar to start a new project.
2. To add a block, select the block from the blocks palette and drag it in the script area.
3. You can also change values in the blocks whenever you need.

## Moving a Sprite

You can move a Sprite by using blocks from the Motion block palette as shown on the right. Here are some of the blocks from this palette that are used to move the Sprite.

*Motion block palette*

- **move 10 steps** : This moves the Sprite 10 steps ahead. The number of steps can be changed by retyping the number in the box.

- **turn ↻ 15 degrees** : This turns the Sprite by 15 degrees clockwise. The number of degrees can be changed by retyping the number in the box.

- **turn ↺ 15 degrees** : This turns the Sprite by 15 degrees anticlockwise. The number of degrees can be changed by retyping the number in the box.

- **point in direction 90▾** : This changes the direction in which the Sprite is pointing. The default is 90 degrees, and this can be changed using the drop-down menu.

- **go to x: 0 y: 0** : This takes your sprite to the specific *x* and *y* coordinates.

- **change x by 10** / **set x to 0** / **change y by 10** / **set y to 0** : This block changes the *x* and *y* coordinates of the Sprite.

## Example project

Let us create a Scratch Project by specifying the Sprite's location on the Stage.

1. Drag the  block from the Events block.

2. Select the blocks from the Motion category, as shown below:

3. Now click the ⚑ button to execute (run) the project and see the movement of the Sprite.

# Adding Sound to a Project

You can make your project exciting by adding sound to it. Add sound to the project either by using the blocks in the **Sound** block palette or by importing sound from the **Sounds** tab.

## Choosing sound from Sound tab

Let us explore different ways of adding sound using the **Sound** tab.

1. Click on the **Sounds** tab at the top of the Scripts Area. A **New sound** pane will appear.

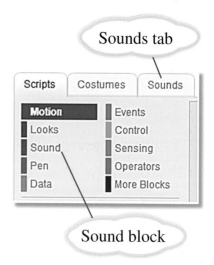

Sounds tab

Sound block

*The Sounds tab and Sound block*

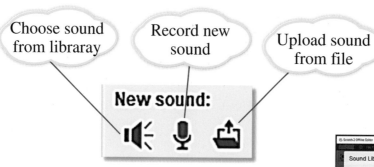

Choose sound from libraray

Record new sound

Upload sound from file

*New Sound section*

2. Under the **New Sound** section, you will find three options as shown above.

3. Click on the **Choose sound from library** button. A **Sound Library** dialog box will appear as shown on the right.

4. Choose any category from the given options – for example, select the **Animal** category and click **OK**.

5. The selected option will be added to the Sound list.

*Selecting the Animal category in the Sound Library*

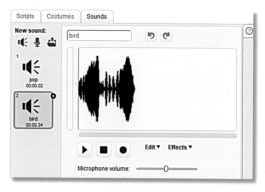

*Selected sound option*

- The selected sound will also be added in the drop-down list of the **play sound** block in the **Sound** tab.

## Record a new sound

To record a new sound follow these steps:

1. Click on the **Record new sound** button in the **Sounds** tab.

2. A **Sound Recorder** pane will appear. It displays three buttons: **Play**, **Stop** and **Record**.

*Sound Recorder pane*

3. Click on the **Record** button to start the recording. The time period of the recording starts increasing, which indicates that the recording has started.

4. Click on the **Pause** button to take a pause in your recording.

5. To play the recording, click on the **Play** button.

**FACT FILE**

Right-click on any block and select **Help**. A short description of the block will appear in the **Help** dialog box.

**TRY THIS**

Create a Sprite of your choice and add sound using the **Sound** block.

135

## Saving a Project

You should always save a project after creating it. The steps for saving a Scratch project are given below.

1. To save a project click on the **File** tab ⟹ **Save as** option from the Menu bar.

2. In the **File name** give the name of the project. The default extension of Scratch files is *.sb2.

*Saving a Scratch project*

## Open an Existing Project

To open an existing project, follow the steps given below.

1. Select **File** tab ⟹ **Open** option from the Menu bar. Insert the name of the file that you want to open. You can also select the project with a mouse from the respective folder.

2. Click on the **Open** button.

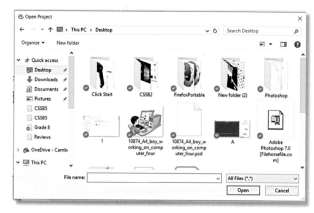

## How to exit from Scratch

To exit from the Scratch window, make sure that you have saved the project.

1. Select **File** tab ⟹ **Quit** option from the Menu bar. It will confirm with you if you have saved the changes to the project before exiting Scratch.

*Opening an existing Scratch project*

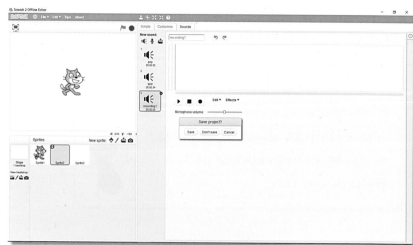

*Exiting from Scratch*

## ACTIVITY

Create a Scratch project by adding a boy, a girl and an animal. Create a story about them by adding sound.

## GLOSSARY

**Scratch** A visual programming language which is based on the dragging and dropping of blocks.

**Sprite** An in-built graphic character in Scratch to which commands can be given to perform actions.

**YOU ARE HERE**

**9**

1. In Scratch, with the help of blocks, the skills of a programming language can be learnt easily.
2. New Sprites can be added in different ways.
3. Blocks are found in various tabs for easy programming.
4. Sound can be added in the project by importing a file or by recording a new sound.
5. Projects must be saved before quitting the application.

## EXERCISE

**A. Fill in the blanks with the correct word.**

1. The default extension of Scratch files is ........................... .

2. Scratch is independent of an ........................... .

3. When we open Scratch, by default the ........................... Sprite appears on the stage.

4. The ........................... is the actual area to draw or perform actions.

5. The ........................... is used to stop the execution of the block.

6. The ........................... bar contains the title of the application currently being used.

## B. Label the following components of the Scratch window.

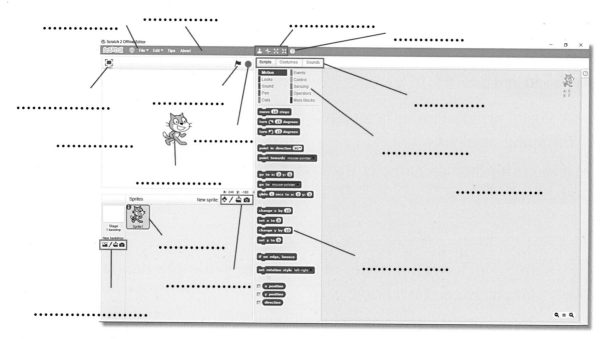

## C. True or false?

1. Sprites cannot be changed in Scratch.

2. The Green flag feature is used to start the execution of all scripts in the project.

3. Scratch is not available for free.

4. The direction of the Sprite can be changed.

5. The collection of step-wise instructions given to a Sprite is called a Script.

## D. Answer the following questions.

1. What is Scratch? Why do we use Scratch?
2. In how many ways can a new Sprite be added to your project?
3. Explain the difference between two types of turn blocks under the Motion category.
4. How can sound be added to your project?
5. Give the steps to save your project.

## LAB WORK

Write a script in Scratch to move the Sprite so that it makes the shape of **C**.

## PROJECT WORK

Record a sound and play it with a new Sprite. Make the Sprite move.

# Scratch 3.0
# Updates

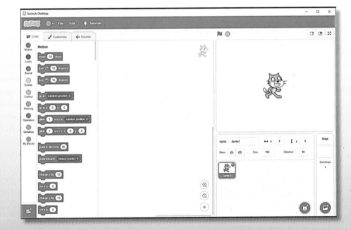

- Scratch 3.0 is the most recent version of Scratch which is also called **Scratch Desktop**. It was released on 2 January 2019.

- The interface of Scratch 3.0 is a complete reimplementation of Scratch 2.0 as shown on the right.

- The major changes in Scratch 3.0 are:

1. The placement of components in the Scratch window is completely different.

2. **Scripts** (in Scratch 2.0) are called **Code** (in Scratch 3.0).

3. Many blocks are in a different order and color. For example, in Scratch 3.0, the Events blocks are the color of the Scratch 2.0 Control blocks, and the color of the Control blocks is lighter than the Events blocks in Scratch 2.0.

4. **More Blocks** (in Scratch 2.0) are called **My Blocks** (in Scratch 3.0).

# Sample Paper

**Tick (✓) the correct option.**

1. **Which of the following is not part of a computer network?**

   a. Process ☐    b. Server ☐    c. Workstation ☐    d. Transmission cables ☐

2. **Identify the correct sentence(s) about a modem used in computer networks.**

   a. It stands for modulator demodulator ☐

   b. It converts data from digital to analogue and vice versa for effective transmission. ☐

   c. Both A and B are correct. ☐

   d. Both A and B are incorrect. ☐

3. **The ....... option from the Start menu is used for executing a file or application directly.**

   a. Accessories ☐    b. All programs ☐    c. Run ☐    d. Gadgets ☐

4. **The On-Screen Keyboard is an important utility program. It is also known as:**

   a. Online keyboard ☐    c. Offline keyboard ☐

   b. Virtual keyboard ☐    d. Soft keyboard ☐

5. **The Control Panel can be used to change settings for Windows. Which of the following setting options is not available in it?**

   a. Keyboard ☐    b. Sound ☐    c. Motherboard ☐    d. Mail ☐

6. **The Region and Language icon of the Control Panel is used for changing the settings of ..........**

   a. the display of languages ☐    b. time ☐    c. date ☐    d. All of these ☐

7. **Which of the following MS Office components is used to create office reports, brochures, business cards, newsletters, etc.**

   a. MS Outlook ☐    b. MS OneNote ☐    c. MS Publisher ☐    d. MS Excel ☐

8. **What is the function of shortcut key F1 in MS Office 2010?**

   a. To close a file ☐                    c. To select the entire text ☐
   b. To access Help ☐                   d. To print a file ☐

9. **In MS Word 2010, where do you find this icon?**

   a. Illustrations group of Insert tab ☐    c. Clipboard group of Insert tab ☐
   b. Illustrations group of Home tab ☐    d. Clipboard group of Home tab ☐

10. **………. is a picture or a graphic image that can be inserted in an MS Word document.**

   a. Custom Art ☐    b. WordArt ☐    c. Clip Art ☐    d. Shapes ☐

11. **Select the correct sentence(s) with reference to MS PowerPoint 2010.**

   a. A theme is a template with a specific design that can be applied to a slide or to the entire presentation. ☐

   c. WordArt are files of general-purpose graphics consisting of animations and cartoons. ☐

   d. All of the above ☐

   b. The user cannot apply a theme with their chosen colors and fonts. ☐

12. **In MS PowerPoint 2010, the Media group from the Insert tab can be used to ……………………**

   a. add a hyperlink to the presentation ☐

   c. add a music file or a movie clip to the presentation ☐

   b. add SmartArt to the presentation ☐

   d. add an MS Word document to the presentation ☐

13. **In MS Excel 2010, ……….. is the column letter and row number that identifies a single cell.**

   a. Cell range ☐    b. Cell reference ☐    c. Cell value ☐    d. Merge cell ☐

**14.** Which feature of MS Excel 2010 allows you to quickly fill the cells with repetitive or sequential data such as chronological dates or numbers or repeated text?

a. Auto Handle ☐   b. Fill Handle ☐   c. Value Fill ☐   d. Auto Fill ☐

**15.** Which of the following is not a governing body of the Internet?

a. American Standard Code for Information Interchange (ASCII) ☐

b. Internet Activities Board (IAB) ☐

c. Internet Engineering Task Force (IETF) ☐

d. Internet Research Task Force (IRTF) ☐

**16.** A modem is a device that allows communication with other computers. The speed of a modem is measured in ........................

a. bytes per second ☐

b. bits per second ☐

c. bits per minute ☐

d. bytes per minute ☐

**17.** Which of the following sentence(s) is/are correct with reference to flowcharts?

a. The analog representation of an algorithm. ☐

b. The logical representation of an algorithm. ☐

c. The graphical representation of an algorithm. ☐

d. The digital representation of an algorithm. ☐

**18.** How can you show a decision using a flowchart?

a. ☐   b. ☐   c. ☐   d. ☐

**19.** In Scratch programming, which of the following tabs help you record new sound?

a. Sound and Recording ☐   b. Sounds ☐   c. Generate sounds ☐   d. Events ☐

**20.** Which of the following statements is correct with reference to Scratch programming?

a. You can add a Sprite in many ways. ☐

b. You can only upload existing sounds in a Scratch project. ☐

c. A Sprite can be moved only once. ☐

d. Scratch projects need to be saved since they are auto-saved. ☐